The Prism Of God

The Prism Of God

Scott Testori

The Prism Of God

All Scripture references are from the Authorized Version (King James Version), unless otherwise noted.

ISBN-13: 978-1533645302
ISBN-10: 1533645302

For additional information and messages, go to:

Strait Gate Education

at

http://www.str8g8ed.com

To all those
who allow the
light of God
to shine
through
them

Contents

Author's Preface

This book is not the product of an extended period of study; yet, at the same time, it is. You see, there's something that I learned a long time ago: the deepest truths in the Word of God are veiled, hidden from the eyes of the unbeliever, as well as from the nominal Christian. Consequently, it's critical that we spend quite some time in studying the Scriptures, if we want to understand them. The more time we spend in the Word, the more we're going to come to understand the Word. Thus, on the one hand, this work is the result of some years of study.

On the other hand, it came to be in just about three months. It started with a message that I did concerning the first Beatitude, which speaks of those who mourn. At that time, I was going to do a series of messages that looked at the Beatitudes; but the Lord changed that. In the middle of April, a seed of another message was planted; that being the relationship between the life of Jesus, and our lives. Then I began to see the connection between the two thoughts; that being that Jesus is our example, our pattern, for becoming a full manifested son of God, and that the Beatitudes as a guide to a change of heart and mind so that we can attain that place. However, it was when He showed me how the fruit of the Spirit fit into this mix that I came to realize that this would take more than just a message or two to even begin to do justice to the subject.

Consequently, this book is intended to show you what the Lord has called us to. I find it somewhat amazing and disconcerting that so many Christians believe that there's a gulf between us and Jesus. By this, I mean that they truly believe that they'll never attain experiential perfection, just like Jesus. They adamantly hold to professing that "we'll never be perfect, because we're human". But, in the words of Jesus, they *"do err, not knowing the Scriptures, nor the power of God" (Matthew 22:29).*

All throughout the Word of God, there are patterns to reveal to us the Father's plans and purposes for a body of believers who will be empowered to fulfill them; and the greatest pattern is Jesus. It's absolutely true that He came to be our substitute, to take our place, and to pay the price for our redemption and salvation. But, He didn't do that strictly to save us, so that we can "make heaven our home". Though that's one aspect of His work, the greater aspect is that He made it possible for us to become just exactly like He was, in every respect!

There's one last thing that I want to say. There are multitudes of books available, and those authors are noted pastors, and/or experts with numerous years' experience in their field of study. Many have doctorates, or PHD's, or are renowned in the Christian, and sometimes in the secular, world. But I have no similar credentials. I don't have the years of training in seminary, nor the practical experience of pastoring a large church. However, I DO have one thing: and that's the Holy Spirit. He's given me a word to share, and I've been sharing it for over thirty years. You see, the Lord doesn't depend upon whether or not we have the physical credentials that the world and, unfortunately, the church, requires. Rather, He's looking for those unrenowned, unrecognized believers, who accept the fact that He's the God of the impossible, and that He'll do what He's said He's going to do. Plain and simple!

Scott Testori
June 10, 2016

The Watchers

Be thou an example of the believers, in word, in conversation, in charity, in spirit, in faith, in purity. (1 Timothy 4:12)

The year was 1787, and the place was Straubing, in the Electorate of Bavaria. Joseph von Fraunhofer was born on March 6th; but, in 1798, at the age of 11, he became an orphan, and started working as an apprentice to a harsh glass maker named Philippe Anton Weichelsberger. Three years later, an incident occurred, which changed the course of Joseph's life forever. The workshop in which he worked collapsed, and buried him in the rubble. Prince-Elector Maximilian Joseph led the rescue operation; and, afterward, provided him with books, as well as forcing Weichelsberger to allow Fraunhofer time to study.

Over the course of time, starting in 1806, he entered an institute which was devoted to glass making, where he discovered how to make the world's finest optical glass. Without going into too much technical detail, in his quest to create the best glass, Fraunhofer ultimately invented the spectroscope in 1814, which breaks down light into its components. And it was during his experiments with this that he discovered 574 dark fixed lines in the solar spectrum, which are actually atomic absorption lines. Like many glass makers in his era, Fraunhofer was poisoned by heavy metal vapors, and died at the young age of 39. But, to this day, those dark absorption lines are called *Fraunhofer lines* in his honor.

What, then, are atomic absorption lines? Well, through the use of a spectroscope, called the science of spectroscopy, the light from a distant object, such as a star, is used to determine what that object is made of. The light passes through the spectroscope, where it's split into its component colors. This, then, lets you see which chemicals are present (the colors which appear), and which ones aren't (the Fraunhofer lines); and that, then, tells you what chemicals are or are not present in the composition of the object.

Why did I bring out what I just did? What does spectroscopy have to do with the things of the Lord? Well, though Christians will say that they believe that ALL things are MADE by God, far too many fail to understand that everything in nature, both upon this earth, as well as to the farthest reaches of the universe, is intricately involved with God and His purposes. They readily admit and profess that God *"created the heaven and the earth" (Genesis 1:1)*, but they fail to recognize the fact that He created them for a reason. He didn't create, just to fill up space. He created, because He has an ultimate, glorious plan for EVERYTHING.

So, there's Christianity, and the belief in creation by God, on one side of the coin; while, on the flip side, there's secular science. And, ironically, the more that they discover "new" things (which really aren't new at all), and attempt to describe them in natural terms, the more that they actually are proving the unfathomable wisdom of the Father. Thus, there's a gulf that exists between the two "sides"; and hardcore Christians reject the viewpoint of hardcore secular scientists, and vice-versa; and they both end up losing out in the long run.

On the one hand, secular science has tried successfully, but far more often, unsuccessfully, to explain away the workings of creation in completely natural terms; and they totally reject anything remotely associated with creation and God. The end result for them is actually hopelessness; because they've refused to understand that there's far more to creation than just what can be seen and explained. On the other hand, many Christians reject the discoveries of scientists, and astronomers, and biologists, and others, based upon the fact that they explain things, in many cases, to the exclusion of God. So, instead of looking at the results of the secular scientists, and, through the guidance of the Holy Spirit, come to understand what the Lord is saying through them, many Christians disregard those discoveries based upon semantics. Therefore, for example, astronomers explain what they know of the workings of the universe in natural terms, and many Christians reject those things because of the failure of the scientists to ascribe those workings to the Almighty. I want to give you a couple of examples here, to show you what I'm talking about.

First: I'm pretty sure that most of us have heard about the "big bang" theory. According to astronomers and other scientists, the entire universe was birthed at this event. Contrarily, Christians adhere to creation by God. Consequently, this is an area where there is a very sharp divide between the two. As I looked at some of the things that are written about the scientific theory, something stood out. So, I looked through some of the books that I wrote, and found the place in "Glory In The Wilderness, Volume One" where I addressed this very issue. Therefore, I want to bring it out again here.

In the beginning God created the heaven and the earth.

And the earth was without form, and void; and darkness was upon the face of the deep. And the Spirit of God

moved upon the face of the waters.
And God said, Let there be light: and there was light. (Genesis 1:1 to 3)

I would tend to say that nearly everyone has heard of the "big bang" theory for the creation of the universe. Well, a number of months ago I saw an article which caught my eye, as well as gave me a hefty portion of food for thought. The article was called, *"What Came Before Creation?"*, and was written by Gregg Easterbrook. It was in the July 20, 1998 issue of "U.S. News & World Report"; and it took me about eight or ten times of reading the article to even BEGIN to grasp what was written. Well, the idea behind the "big bang" theory is that, at one time, all of the matter that makes up the universe was compressed into a single place, locked in an atom of unthinkable mass. Then, suddenly, this atom exploded, sending all of that matter outward, and forming the stars, planets, and everything else that now exists. Well, since then, various physicists have come up with various theories, every one of them mind-boggling. I wouldn't attempt to explain these things here, simply because most all of them I won't even pretend to understand.

There is one idea, however, that I found MOST interesting, in light of what I'm writing about. It's called the "inflation" theory. The idea behind this is that, before the big bang, there was what is called a "false vacuum", which was, very simply, a transparent area with almost nothing in it. One of the things that WAS in it, however, was a potential for vast amounts of "virtual" particles; subatomic (smaller than an atom) units that sometimes pop out of nowhere. Every now and then, this "false vacuum" underwent routine minor fluctuations, or changes. But then, a sensational fluctuation hit the vacuum, and everything came unglued! This would be what science called the "big bang"; whereupon, the "false vacuum" gave rise to this universe! Consequently, the universe that we're in right now is a daughter of the "false vacuum". And there are a couple of astrophysicists who claim that this wasn't an isolated occurrence, but could happen anywhere in the universe, and at any time; something that they call "inflation". And one physicist, Alexander Vilenkin, of Tufts University, believes that what came before the "big bang" creation event was nothing in the literal sense.

Okay, now, we know that, according to the Scriptures, God spoke the worlds into existence supernaturally. BUT, who says that these physicists are TOTALLY out of line with the Spirit in their thinking? Don't get me wrong: I'm not saying that they're absolutely right in their theories. What I AM saying, though, is that we can't box God in, and them out. I mean, God is God, and He can do whatever He wants to any way He wants to! And all down through the Word of God we read of Him using NATURAL events to work His supernatural purposes. For example, most of the plagues that came upon Egypt by the hand of Moses were natural events that occurred in the land at various times. The supernatural part of it was that they all occurred at once, and at the command of Moses. And, if you read the Word carefully, you'll see that there were numerous occasions of the supernatural being worked out through the natural!

Now, I said that to say this. Suppose the "inflation" theory is a shadow of reality? So, let me put forth a scenario to you. Don't forget: this is only a theory. I can't prove it, and you don't have to believe it. But seek the Lord prayerfully concerning it.

We know that the divine Triune, the Father, the Word, and the Spirit, has ALWAYS existed. They had no beginning, and they have no end. And that place that they inhabited before the existence of all things was called the eternal spiritual realm; something of which we have no possible ability to comprehend with our finite minds. This is what the physicists, in their attempts to explain the unexplainable, have called a "false vacuum". After an untold length of time (if I can use that term, since time didn't exist), and according to the Father's purposes, the Word came forth: *"Let there be light"*. And with that Word came a change in the cosmos of that first spiritual realm. THIS is what the physicists call that sensational fluctuation, or change, when everything came unglued. This is what they call the "big bang"!

Let me tell you what, according to the physicists, happened when the "big bang" occurred. First came the "era of inflation", when the universe inflated; kind of like what happens to something when it gets blown up. This, however, took only one trillionth of a second! Well, immediately after that was when protons, neutrons, and other subatomic (smaller than an atom) particles were formed, resulting in a dense fog of matter and radiation. This occurred one hundred thousandth of a second after the bang. One hundred seconds after this - and this is the goody - helium and other light elements formed! God gave us the Reader's Digest condensed version of it.

And God said, Let there be light: and there was light. (Genesis 1:3)

<><><><><><><><><><><><><><><>

In this case, many Christians tend to throw out the concept of the "big bang" theory, without taking into account that those who are ignorant of God and His power and majesty are attempting, to the best of their ability, to explain things that He created. This actually is not much different than when Paul, while in Athens, Greece, stood on Mars' hill, and said, *"Ye men of Athens, I perceive that in all things ye are too superstitious. For as I passed by, and beheld your devotions, I found an altar with this inscription, TO THE UNKNOWN GOD. Whom therefore ye ignorantly worship, him declare I unto you" (Acts 17:22 and 23).* Paul didn't reject them, nor did he berate them for their failure to recognize God. Rather, he declared the truth to them. You see, as Christians, we have a greater responsibility to bear with the ignorance of those who don't know the Lord, than it is for those who don't know the Lord to bear with us who do.

A second example that I want to bring out has to do with one simple word that immediately drives Christians away, and shuts them down. That word is: Zodiac". As soon as Christians hear that word, they instantly think of all of the negative ideas that the enemy has woven into what the Lord created. But, again, we need to recognize the difference between the things of the Lord, and the things of the enemy, and not lump the two together. Consider the following portion of Scripture.

> *Canst thou bind the sweet influences of Pleiades, or loose the bands of Orion?*
>
> *Canst thou bring forth Mazzaroth in his season? or canst thou guide Arcturus with his sons?*
>
> *Knowest thou the ordinances of heaven? canst thou set the dominion thereof in the earth? (Job 38:31 to 33)*

Don't you realize that God created what has been called the Zodiac? And don't you realize that God created all of the constellations? And, again, don't you realize that it was God Who established true astrology? It was astrologers, the wise men from the east, who read the signs in the heavens, and understood the import of that particular star that they followed to find Jesus. And it was God Who established the pattern of the constellations, starting with Virgo, "the Virgin", and ending with Leo, "the Lion", to display His Gospel in the heavens, for everyone to see; for Jesus was born of a virgin, and is seated at the right hand of the Father as King of kings.

With that said, do you know what the Lord is showing us through spectroscopy, and through atomic absorption lines? Again, the basic explanation of this is that all of the components of the light that come from a particular star reveal what the star is made of; and the *Fraunhofer lines*, the dark lines, reveal what is missing. Thus, every believer has been endued with a measure of the Spirit of God, for the purpose of empowering us to become like Jesus. It's not to do great and marvelous works, although those can be a result; and it's not to turn the entire world upside down. There's a time when those things will happen; but, for the majority, that time isn't now. Rather, again, we've received the Holy Spirit, so that He can begin to work within us, and to shape us into the image of the firstborn Son, Jesus Christ.

What about those *Fraunhofer lines*, as well as those things that are revealed through the spectroscope? Very simply, we're being watched. Yes, there are those around us, whether it's family, or friends, or acquaintances of some sort, or even total strangers, who are affected, not so much by our words, as by our actions. And what they see or hear shapes their bigger concepts of

Christianity. But, in a way of which we have very little insight, there are those around us who are watching us; and we're dreadfully blind to this far too often.

> *Wherefore seeing we also are compassed about with so great a cloud of witnesses, let us lay aside every weight, and the sin which doth so easily beset us, and let us run with patience the race that is set before us, (Hebrews 12:1)*

Those witnesses whom Paul was writing about were those whom he had spoken of in the previous chapter. They're those who *"died in faith, not having received the promises (Hebrews 11:13)*. But, as I was looking at this in connection with the fact that there are those who are watching us, there's something that came to me. And, for this, I want to give you some food for thought. Take a look at a couple of portions of Scripture.

> *I knew a man in Christ above fourteen years ago, (whether in the body, I cannot tell; or whether out of the body, I cannot tell: God knoweth;) such an one caught up to the third heaven. (2 Corinthians 12:2)*

> *After this I looked, and, behold, a door was opened in heaven: and the first voice which I heard was as it were of a trumpet talking with me; which said, Come up hither, and I will shew thee things which must be hereafter.*
>
> *And immediately I was in the*

spirit: and, behold, a throne was set in heaven, and one sat on the throne. (Revelation 4:1 and 2)

Both of these portions of Scripture speak, one directly, and one by implication, about a realm in the Spirit called the third heaven. That, then, means one thing in particular: since there's a third heaven, then there HAS to be a first and a second heaven, as well. So, what about them? Well, we know that the third heaven is the abode of the angels, and the spirits of the faithful; and the first heaven is the physical universe, and is the place of the sun, the moon, the stars, and every bit of the universe. That, then, brings us to the second heaven. Think, now. Since the first heaven is the natural one, and the third heaven is the abode of the angels and of the spirits of the faithful, then what is the second heaven? In essence, it's a realm that exists between the two; and it's the dwelling place of all of the powers of darkness. After all, those powers are not visible in the natural realm, although they have limited access to it, and they have no access to the realms of light, unless specifically allowed there by the Father. In other words, the second heaven is an intermediate realm between the first and the third heavens.

The reason that I've said what I have is to bring out something that may or may not have occurred to you. You see, the number three is a major number in God's economy. First and foremost, God is actually a triune being: the Father, the Son, and the Holy Spirit. The ark that Noah was commanded to build, which was for the purpose of the continuation of the creation, had three floors in it. The tabernacle, which was the pattern of all that Moses saw in the spiritual realm, was constructed with the outer court, the holy place, and the most holy place. The Scriptures were divided into three groups: the Torah (the five books of Moses), the Nevi'im (the Prophets), and the Kethuvim (the Writings). And, then again, the Scriptures as we know them today in Christianity, have been divided into three: the Old Testament, the New Testament, and the link between the two, called the Gospels. I could go on, but there's no need, because I believe that you can understand what I'm saying.

That, then, is pointing to, again, naturally, three things: first, the three heavens; second, the three groups of watchers; and third, those three things of which we are composed: body, soul and spirit. Not only are we compassed about with a great cloud of faithful witnesses dwelling in the third heaven, but we are also compassed about with a great host of enemies, which dwell in the second heaven. Along with that, we're compassed about with people who dwell upon the earth. So, each of these groups have an effect on our spiritual walk.

The third group, who are people who dwell upon the earth, have very limited, and, many times, nonexistent insight into the spiritual realms. They watch our actions, and listen to our words, and they judge us accordingly. Thus, the only real effect that people can have on our spiritual walk is a physical one. The next group, the powers of darkness which dwell in the second heaven, also have limited insight into our true spiritual walk. They see more than people do, but very little of what the Lord and those heavenly witnesses do. Consequently, the only influence that they can have upon us is to attempt to sway our thoughts and desires. Finally, it's that great company of faithful witnesses who dwell in the third heaven who are praying for us, and encouraging us spiritually, both of which we're really quite unaware. And it's these who have the most effect upon the most critical aspect of our eternity.

Can you see, then, what the Lord is showing us? Again, there are three heavens, there are three groups, and there are three aspects to us: body, soul, and spirit. The third group, composed of natural, physical people who are dwelling upon the natural, physical earth, can have a limited effect only upon our natural, physical bodies. The second group, which are the powers of darkness, also have a limited effect upon us, but in the realm of the soul. Just as our soul is what controls the natural man through our wants and desires, so the powers of darkness can only influence that part of us, in an attempt to interfere with our spiritual growth. The third group, which are those heavenly witnesses, have the greatest effect upon our spirit, and are doing everything in their power to help us to attain what the Father has called us to.

Briefly, then: man, in the physical, first heavenly realm, can only influence our physical body; the powers of darkness, in the second heavenly realm, can only influence our soul; and that great cloud of witnesses, in the third heavenly realm, can influence our spirit. And, though we have been given authority over our body and our soul through the Spirit, and, by extension, authority over the limited authority of man and of the powers of darkness, so that our spirit affects our body and soul, still, if we allow either of the other two to have authority over our spirit, it can have a negative impact on our spiritual growth.

So, there's something that we have to remember: the Father has given us authority over the influence of man and of the powers of darkness by reason of His Holy Spirit, Who dwells within us. And there's something else that we need to remember: we have a choice. The more that we CHOOSE to allow the Holy Spirit,

Who dwells within us, to have authority in our life, the less authority our flesh and the enemy will have.

We are, in a sense, a spiritual prism. The Lord has drawn us to Himself, not so much to give us the opportunity to "make heaven our eternal home", but, rather, to learn how to become His sons in the exact likeness of Jesus Christ. And, according to Jesus Himself, His entire life was dedicated to manifesting the Father to the creation. He was God's perfect prism, reflecting and dispersing the light of the nature of the Father to all with whom He came in contact; and, actually, it's still ongoing. We, too, are saved to be the same things: God's prism, reflecting and dispersing the light of the nature of the Father to the creation.

There's a difference between Jesus as He was, and us as we are right now. That's perfectly understandable, and perfectly acceptable. Those differences can be summed up in two words: Fraunhofer lines. Jesus had none. He had no darkness within Him; but He manifested the absolutely perfect light of the Father, with no lack, and no darkness. We, on the other hand, are laden with spiritual Fraunhofer lines, even though His Spirit dwells within us. But, again, the more that we <u>CHOOSE</u> to allow the light of the Spirit of the Father to manifest through us, the less Fraunhofer lines we'll have. True: to complete this, the Father is going to have to do another special work. However, for the present, we need to consciously surrender the authority of our lives to the Holy Spirit. After all, we're God's workmanship; and He intends to use us for His greatest eternal purposes.

For now, we're being watched.

The Plumb Line

Thus he shewed me: and, behold, the Lord stood upon a wall made by a plumbline, with a plumbline in his hand.

And the Lord said unto me, Amos, what seest thou? And I said, A plumbline. Then said the Lord, Behold, I will set a plumbline in the midst of my people Israel: I will not again pass by them any more: (Amos 7:7 and 8)

In the previous chapter, I had spoken about the fact that we have been called to be made into the exact image of Jesus Christ, and that the Holy Spirit dwells within us to accomplish that purpose. That may seem impossible, when we look at ourselves; but it's completely possible when we realize that the God Whom we serve is the God of the impossible. And why should it seem so strange that God would want to literally perfect us? After all, that's what He had intended when He created man in the first place. Just because so many Christians lack the faith to believe for it doesn't mean that God can't do it. It just means that THEY don't think He can.

But He can!

And He will!

There are, however, some requirements, some responsibilities, that rest with us. You see, grace is offered to us as a free gift. There's nothing that we can do to merit it, other than to ask God for it. It's something of which we're totally unworthy. And the anointing of the Holy Spirit is also ours for the asking. But, to attain experientially to the image of Jesus requires that we be willing to surrender our life to Him, and to allow Him to be Lord over us. This is an interactive relationship that the Lord would love to have with every one who claims to be His follower. There are some who say that there's nothing that we can do in any way whatsoever to attain to Jesus, and that He's done it all. They say that every believer has attained that place when they accepted Him as their Savior. However, there are a number of Scriptures that contradict that idea.

> *And he that taketh not his cross, and followeth after me, is not worthy of me. (Matthew 10:38)*

> *What shall we say then? Shall we continue in sin, that grace may abound? God forbid. How shall we, that are dead to sin, live any longer therein? (Romans 6:1 and 2)*

> *Let not sin therefore reign in your mortal body, that ye should obey it in the lusts thereof. (Romans 6:12)*

> *There is therefore now no condemnation to them which are in Christ Jesus, who walk not after the flesh, but after the Spirit. (Romans 8:1)*

> *For they that are after the flesh do mind the things of the flesh; but they that are after the Spirit, the things of the Spirit. (Romans 8:5)*

> *He that overcometh, the same shall be clothed in white raiment; and I*

will not blot out his name out of the book of life, but I will confess his name before my Father, and before his angels. (Revelation 3:5)

I only just barely touched on a few portions of Scripture, but they all are bringing forth the same message. You see, Jesus, nor Paul, nor John, ever made allowance for sin. Yes, it's true that every one of us, as believers, are prone to sin. But, I haven't read anywhere in the Word of God where the Lord, nor any of the writers, ever accepted a life of sin from anyone who claimed to be a follower of Jesus. Instead, every one of them, according to the Spirit of God, threw down the gauntlet. They made no allowance for sin; and they actually went as far as to declare that those who have become a child of God have no business allowing sin in their lives! Far too many Christians today have chosen, and have tried to justify, the path of least resistance. As a matter of fact, we're all guilty of that at one time or another. But, again: the Lord has commanded us to turn to Him at every step, and to allow Him to have control over our lives to the point that we don't fall into sin; not because we shouldn't, but because we would rather please Him, and serve Him. He should be the reason that we do whatever we do; and He should be the focus of our lives. The Father was the focus of Jesus' life, and it should be the same for us.

Now, before you start saying that it's impossible to get to that point, don't let those words come out of your mouth! Know this, and rehearse it to yourself, until it becomes so ingrained in your heart and mind that it becomes a natural part of you: what you say is what you become! You see, our words imprint our mind with ideas, which then find a place in our heart, and, ultimately, shapes our life. I know that what we see has the same effect; but words tend to have a power that the visual doesn't have. That's why James, through the Holy Spirit, wrote, in the third chapter of his letter, not about what we see with our eyes, nor what we listen to with our ears, but, rather, about what we speak with our tongue.

> *For in many things we offend all. If any man offend not in word, the same is a perfect man, and able also to bridle the whole body.*
>
> *Behold, we put bits in the horses' mouths, that they may obey us; and we turn about their whole body.*
>
> *Behold also the ships, which though they be so great, and are driven of fierce winds, yet are they turned about with a very small helm, whithersoever the governor listeth.*
>
> *Even so the tongue is a little member, and boasteth great things. Behold, how great a matter a little fire kindleth!*
>
> *And the tongue is a fire, a world of iniquity: so is the tongue among our members, that it defileth the whole body, and setteth on fire the course of nature; and it is set on fire of hell. (James 3:2 to 6)*

Now, there's something in this that may not be too apparent; but, if you think about it, you'll understand what I'm about to say. Our tongue can do damage with words that don't appear to be harmful or negative. Consider this. One of the statements that seems to stem from humility is: "I'm just a sinner saved by grace". As a matter of fact, there's a Gospel song that puts that forth; and I'm in full agreement with the truth of it. Every single believer can attest to that; and, if we don't, we risk standing in opposition to the Word of God. But, where I'm going with this is how often it's used, and, many times, the reason that it's used.

You see, every time that we make the statement that "I'm just a sinner saved by grace", we're reaffirming the fact that we're a sinner. On the surface, that appears to be our affirmation that we're unworthy of all that we've received from God through the sacrifice of Jesus; and that keeps that thought alive and active in our mind and heart. But, the result is that it tends to cause us to determine that we'll never amount to anything more than being "a sinner saved by grace"! It establishes within our mind that it's impossible for us to attain to the express image of Jesus Christ. In short, it puts the promise of Romans 8:29, when understood as it was intended to be understood, out of reach.

Along with that, the acclamation seems to be used quite often to justify why we tend to continue in sin. Instead of attempting to walk as the Lord requires us to walk, which is without sin (and we DO have that ability, if we have the Holy Spirit dwelling within us), we fall back upon a couple of things: "We're just a sinner saved by (and depending upon) grace", and "we're still just only human". I've heard it said that God doesn't require His followers to live a perfect, sinless, life, because Jesus took our place there, as well as on the cross. And I've heard it said that, as long as we're dwelling in our humanity, then we'll never be perfect, simply because of our inherent Adamic nature. But, that train of thought does two things: it makes the Word of God a lie, and it makes the Holy Spirit impotent!

It's a fact that we have all inherited the Adamic sin nature, and there's nothing that we can do to change that. But that doesn't mean that sin is inevitable. Rather, it means that we have been born with the tendency to sin. Even though sin results in death, it's not like a disease over which we have no real control. Cancer, for example, is not something that we choose to accept or reject. Sin, on the other hand, is a choice. We either obey the Lord, or we obey our flesh and the enemy. Jesus didn't live a sinless life because He was God incarnate. Remember: He willingly laid aside His divinity when He took upon Himself flesh, so that any person dwelling in flesh could do what He did. Jesus lived a sinless life because of His obedience to the Father. And, the more we obey the Father, the more we'll simply not sin. To say that the Holy Spirit can't bring us to that place is to say that, even if we obey Him fully, He still doesn't have the ability to overcome our flesh. That's a lie that the enemy has been using to try to get the believers to stop *"press[ing] toward the mark for the prize of the high calling of God in Christ Jesus" (Philippians 3:14)*!

Easy?

Not at all!

Possible?

Yes!

I want to say a couple of things here concerning our tongue, and what James wrote about. In the Word of God, according to Paul, there are two kinds of tongues.

> *Though I speak with the tongues of men and of angels . . . (1 Corinthians 13:1)*

> *For he that speaketh in an un-*

known tongue speaketh not unto men, but unto God: for no man understandeth him; howbeit in the spirit he speaketh mysteries. (1 Corinthians 14:2)

There are tongues which can be understood by someone somewhere in the world; and then there are tongues which belong to no man. Those are the unknown tongues, which Paul referred to as the tongues of angels. But, why, under the anointing of the Holy Spirit, call them *"tongues of angels"*? You'd think that he would have called it the tongue of the Holy Spirit; but he didn't. Is there really no difference, or is there something more that many don't realize? I had put forth a few thoughts about this once before; but there's a little bit more that I want to bring out, as well as touching upon another point that I had also addressed in a previous writing. And, as with other thoughts that I put forth, they're food for thought, and for your consideration.

First: getting to the *"tongues of angels"*. I believe that there was a reason that Paul called the unknown tongues that; and it goes back to a time in the far distant past. One thing we DO know is that, because there was a rebellion amongst the angels, led by Lucifer, then it means that, at one time before that, there was an initial unity amongst them. And one of the things about that unity was that there was one language. In other words, all of the angels spoke with one language. Yet, even though it was a language, it wasn't like humans speak. Rather, it was a spiritual one. Nonetheless, that which they "spoke" was one, as a result of their unity.

There was, as I said, a rebellion in that high, heavenly realm. A large number of angels (traditionally, about a third part of them), led by Lucifer, decided that they were worthy of more than what the Father had determined for them; and their decision was the rebellion which cost them dearly and eternally. As a result, the Father did something that He repeated in a similar situation.

> *And the whole earth was of one language, and of one speech.*
>
> *And it came to pass, as they journeyed from the east, that they found a plain in the land of Shinar; and they dwelt there.*
>
> *And they said one to another, Go to, let us make brick, and burn them thoroughly. And they had brick for stone, and slime had they for morter.*
>
> *And they said, Go to, let us build us a city and a tower, whose top may reach unto heaven; and let us make us a name, lest we be scattered abroad upon the face of the earth.*
>
> *And the Lord came down to see the city and the tower, which the children of men builded.*
>
> *And the Lord said, Behold, the people is one, and they have all one language; and this they begin to do: and now nothing will be restrained from them, which they have imagined to do.*
>
> *Go to, let us go down, and there confound their language, that they may not understand one another's speech. (Genesis 11:1 to 7)*

In response to the rebellion in heaven, He drove

the rebels out, and then confounded the "language" which all the rest of the angels "spoke". Thus, I believe that, whereas it once was a universal, singular, spiritual language, it now is *"tongues of angels"*. What I'm getting at has to do with the following two portions of Scriptures; the one that I mentioned above, *"howbeit in the spirit he speaketh mysteries (1 Corinthians 14:2)*, and the following two:

> *Unto whom it was revealed, that not unto themselves, but unto us they did minister the things, which are now reported unto you by them that have preached the Gospel unto you with the Holy Ghost sent down from heaven; which things the angels desire to look into. (1 Peter 1:12)*

> *To the intent that now unto the principalities and powers in heavenly places might be known by the church the manifold wisdom of God. (Ephesians 3:10)*

With all that said, I want to tell you what I'm seeing concerning our speaking with the tongues of angels. Again: this is for your consideration. In essence, when the Lord baptizes us with the Holy Ghost, and we begin to speak in tongues, we're given one of the heavenly languages which belong to certain angels. Consequently, when we speak in tongues, we *"speak[eth] mysteries"* to those angels, so that it makes known to them *"the manifold wisdom of God"*, which they've *"desire[d] to look into"*.

There's another point that I want to bring out

here concerning speaking with tongues; and it's in light of what James wrote. Take another look at this particular Scripture.

> *For in many things we offend all. If any man offend not in word, the same is a perfect man, and able also to bridle the whole body. (James 3:2)*

That's the reason that the Lord uses speaking in an unknown tongue of angels as the evidence of receiving the baptism in the Holy Spirit. If His Spirit is able to gain control of our tongue, He can gain control of our entire being: body, soul and spirit.

The Holy Spirit performs various operations in each of our lives, but He has one primary purpose; and that is to enable us to become exactly like Jesus. To do this, He's constantly speaking to us, and directing us, and prompting us according to the Word of God. You see, there will NEVER be a conflict between the guidance of the Holy Spirit and the Word of God. And, if we truly want to attain to that high and holy place of being like Jesus, then we'd better settle one thing within ourselves: though the Holy Spirit is called "the Comforter", most of what He speaks is not what we consider to be words of comfort, but, rather, words *"for doctrine, for reproof, for correction, for instruction in righteousness" (2 Timothy 3:16).*

Do you know why? Well, it seems that the focus of Christians, primarily in this country, is a bit lopsided. The bulk of the messages from preachers and teachers is how God loves us, and how all believers are His children, and how He wants to give everything that He possesses to His children. I don't have one bit to say against that, because all of it is absolutely true. But, there's something that keeps coming back to me; and that's the Scripture that I just mentioned concerning the purpose of the Word of God. In essence, Jesus, and Paul, and Peter, and James, as well as the early church fathers, and the prophets of old, all threw the gauntlet down. Some of what they brought forth was, indeed, about the love that the Father has for His people, and for all people; but the majority of their messages were intended to guide the people from the path of death and destruction that they were walking, and into the way of life.

We can see all throughout Scripture something that is summarized in the following: *"As it is written, There is none righteous, no, not one" (Romans 3:10)*. Another way of saying that is, *"There is none upright, no, not one"*.

Enter the plumb line.

The concept of a plumb line is very simple. A small weight of some kind is attached to a string or twine, and is suspended, so that it hangs straight. This is used to assure that a wall is vertically straight, regardless of the terrain upon which it is built. It's used in the natural, and it's used in the spiritual. You see, the Lord is in the process of building His temple, *"a spiritual house, an holy priesthood" (1 Peter 2:5)*; being built upon Jesus Christ, the chief Cornerstone. And, since God *"did predestinate [us] to be conformed to the image of his Son" (Romans 8:29)*, then it means that all of the "stones" within this temple will be uniform in every aspect. Well, the Cornerstone was measured by the Father, and was declared to be worthy, and those saints that have gone on have attained that place. However, there are those who are alive, and are striving to be accounted worthy; because, in this realm in which we dwell, we're in a constant battle with our Adamic nature. As an aside, it's tragic that not all of those who claim that they're followers of Jesus are fighting the good fight!

Thus, there's something that we need to realize. The Lord said, *"I will not again pass by them any more: (Amos 7:8)*. What He's saying, very simply, is that the time of His winking at our transgressions is fast coming to a close! And that means that the day of grace is fast coming to a close! Now, grace is what God has extended to those who are His followers, while mercy extends to those who aren't. But, whether it's grace or mercy, God is doing one thing in particular: He's measuring us with His plumb line.

So, just what is God's plumb line?

It's really not very difficult to understand.

Jesus Christ is the plumb line.

Everything that the Father is doing, and everything that He wants to do in us, is based upon one thing: manifesting His Kingdom through Jesus Christ. That's been His intention and His purpose from before He created anything. And, as I said before, this high and holy calling is impossible for us to attain by ourselves; but it's most definitely possible when we depend upon the Holy Spirit Who dwells within us.

We need to understand that this will not be attained by the nominal Christian, nor the spiritually lax, nor the faint of heart. Rather, even though it will be the work of the Holy Spirit, it will be a work that will be accomplished in those who are willing to make coming into the likeness of Jesus their sole desire, their number one priority, no matter what it takes, and no matter how long it takes.

The Firstborn

There are an estimated 3,573 promises in the Word of God; and, according to many Christians: "Every promise in the Word is mine". Now, that sounds encouraging, and it seems to show a God Who is willing, and has the ability, to bless His people abundantly. Y'know what? He IS able to bless every one of us more abundantly than we can ever imagine.

But, if you can handle it, every promise in the Word is NOT mine! Now, before you start thinking that I'm trying to put a damper on what God has said, I want to tell you that I'm not. What I AM doing, which far too many Christians fail to do, is to look at what the Lord has really said, not just what we'd like to think He said. God expects us to have reality faith. In other words, He doesn't want us to have faith for anything and everything, based upon traditions and selfish desires; but, He wants us to know what He's promised, to whom He's promised it, the time that He's promised it will come, and what it takes to receive those promises. If we fall for that "name it and claim it" fallacy, then we'll ultimately guarantee ourselves that we'll be the ones who'll be seated *"the one on [Jesus'] right hand, and the other on the left, in [His] kingdom" (Matthew 20:21)*. With that said, to show you exactly what I'm talking about, take a look at the following portions of Scripture.

> *And it is appointed unto men once to die, but after this the judgment: (Hebrews 9:27)*

> *Behold, I shew you a mystery; We shall not all sleep, but we shall all be changed,*

> *In a moment, in the twinkling of an eye, at the last trump: for the trumpet shall sound, and the dead shall be raised incorruptible, and we shall be changed. (1 Corinthians 15:51 and 52)*

These both are part of the Word of the Lord to us, and they both are absolute truth. Now, we know that the Lord doesn't contradict Himself; yet, at first glance, the two seem to be exceedingly contradictory. But that's impossible! So, which is it? The Lord has established a spiritual law that promises that death has been appointed to every person. However, if that was true, with no exceptions whatsoever, then the promise that there will be those who remain at the coming of the Lord would be a contradiction! Along with that, there would be no accounting for Enoch and Elijah. Yet, in contrast, since there WILL be those whom the Lord has promised will remain, or be alive, at His coming, then that stands in complete contradiction to the appointment of death to every person! One thing that we can count on, though, is that the Word of God does NOT contradict itself at ANY point.

What this shows us is the sovereignty of God. He has full authority over every spiritual and natural law; and He can't be boxed in. Yes: death is the destiny of every person because of the rebellion of our first parents. But that hasn't stopped the Lord. He chose, for His own purposes, to intervene in the lives of Enoch and Elijah, and He's determined to intervene in the lives of that company of sons who will be alive at the coming of Jesus. That brings me to another portion of Scripture.

> *For whom he did foreknow, he also did predestinate to be conformed to*

> *the image of his Son, that he might be the firstborn among many brethren. (Romans 8:29)*

That portion of Scripture has been quoted so often, and by so many believers, that it's become one that almost everyone can recite it verbatim. This is one of the great promises that the Father has given in His Word, and it's something that WILL come to pass. Though it's a glorious promise, does that mean that it's for every follower of the Lord? Sadly, far too many think so.

But, again: not every single promise in the Word of God is to every single believer; and that goes for Romans 8:29, as well. The Lord decides which promises He'll grant to each of His people, and it has nothing to do with what we want. We can't pray it into being, nor can we faith it into being; and, contrary to the teaching in some circles, we can't "name it and claim it". For example:

- Moses prayed that he might be able to enter the promised land after he had delivered and had led the children of Israel for forty years, but the Lord denied him.

- David prayed for the life of his first son with Bathsheba, but the Lord denied him.

- Paul prayed that he might be delivered from what he called the thorn in his side, but the Lord denied him.

- Jesus prayed, in the garden, that there might be another way of fulfilling the Father's purposes, but, with His submission, the Lord denied Him.

So, getting to Romans 8:29, there's something that we need to realize; and it has to do with what I had called reality faith. How does it read?

> *For whom he did foreknow, he also did predestinate to be conformed to the image of his Son, that he might be the firstborn among MANY brethren. (Romans 8:29)*

It doesn't say *"ALL brethren"*, but *"MANY"*. And another portion reads: *"MANY be called, but FEW chosen" (Matthew 20:16)*. Yet again, the tribe of Levi was chosen from out of the twelve to minister to the tabernacle; and certain chosen ones from out of the tribe of Levi to minister as priests within the tabernacle. Then, too, the apostles were the chosen of the Lord from out of the disciples who followed Jesus. What I'm saying is that each believer is called to fulfill something in the Lord's body; and with that calling come certain promises. In other words, not every promise in the Word of God belongs to every believer; but every promise which belongs to a particular calling belongs to the believer who is called to that calling.

Now, I want to bring out something here that I've brought out previously in the book that I wrote, called *"The Prize Unfolding"*. As I said at the beginning of that writing: these things are for your consideration, concerning what I see as something that the Lord has made possible. So, here's the fifth chapter from the book, called *"The Mark, And The Prize"*.

> *Brethren, I count not myself to*

have apprehended: but this one thing I do, forgetting those things which are behind, and reaching forth unto those things which are before,

I press toward the mark for the prize of the high calling of God in Christ Jesus. (Philippians 3:13 and 14)

In this last chapter, there are just two things that I want to look at, and both are actually part of one. As you can see, Paul was saying that he was pressing for one thing, which he called the mark, so that he could qualify for the second, which he called the prize. And, as I looked over a number of things that have been written concerning the mark and the prize, I noticed one thing that many of them have in common: they seem to come short of the glory that God has promised for those who choose to dedicate themselves completely to Him and His purposes. Now, I'm not discounting those things that have been written, because they're all good. What I AM saying is that the Lord wants to open our spiritual vision beyond the point where many tend to focus. Christians have this habit of putting God in a box, and limiting Him; while He's searching for those who will allow Him to do ALL that He's said that He'll do.

The Mark.

With that, consider "the mark". That's the goal to be reached, to make us eligible to attain "the prize". What, then, is "the mark"? Well, that goes right along with the preceding verse.

Not as though I had already attained, either were already perfect: but I follow after, if that I may apprehend that for which also I am apprehended of Christ Jesus. (Philippians 3:12)

What was Paul apprehended of Christ Jesus for? There's a reason that Paul wrote the twelfth verse the way he did. You see, he knew that the Lord had apprehended him for one particular reason; and that was to be made into the likeness of the Son of God. He was apprehended to attain perfection. Granted, Paul knew that he hadn't reached that place; but he was still striving to reach it. His whole desire and purpose was to come into the likeness of Jesus Christ.

So, what does that say to us today? Very simply, the Lord is searching for those who will attain the place that Paul was seeking to attain. What did Paul write?

For whom he did foreknow, he also did predestinate to be conformed to the image of his Son, that he might be the firstborn among many brethren. (Romans 8:29)

Paul tells us that Jesus was the first one of a company of believers who will be exactly like He was, with absolutely no difference. I'm not talking about almost like Him, or pretty close to being like Him, but I'm talking about <u>EXACTLY</u> like Him in <u>EVERY</u> aspect. He was the example of what a true son of God was like; and there will be others who will follow after His example.

There's something that I want to say here, and it flies in the face of what the vast majority of Christians believe, and what is preached and taught by the ministry which, according to Ephesians 4:12, is supposed to be guiding the saints into perfection. Take a look at the following portions of Scripture.

> *Be ye therefore perfect, even as your Father which is in heaven is perfect. (Matthew 5:48)*

> *The disciple is not above his master: but every one that is perfect shall be as his master. (Luke 6:40)*

> *That they all may be one; as thou, Father, art in me, and I in thee, that they also may be one in us: that the world may believe that thou hast sent me.*
>
> *And the glory which thou gavest me I have given them; that they may be one, even as we are one:*
>
> *I in them, and thou in me, that they may be made perfect in one; and that the world may know that thou hast sent me, and hast loved them, as thou hast loved me. (John 17:21 to 23)*

What are those Scriptures saying? Well, according to what has always been taught, they mean things such as being perfect in spirit, or being perfect in Jesus Christ. And, yes, I fully agree with those ideas. But, I have a question for you. What's so difficult to believe that, when Jesus said that His true followers will be perfect, that He meant exactly that?! Is God's Spirit, Who dwells within us, so impotent that He can't bring those who submit to Him into the same perfection of our example, the firstborn of many brethren? Why do so many who claim to be preachers and teachers of God's Word exalt the fact that He can save to the uttermost, but then diminish Him by saying that He can't bring us into the same perfection as Jesus Christ?! Take a look at the following portion of Scripture.

> *If we say that we have no sin, we deceive ourselves, and the truth is not in us.*
>
> *If we confess our sins, he is faithful and just to forgive us our sins, and to cleanse us from all unrighteousness.*
>
> *If we say that we have not sinned, we make him a liar, and his word is not in us.*
>
> *My little children, these things write I unto you,* ***that ye sin not****. (1 John 1:8 to 10, 2:1)*

There's something that a lot of Christians fail to understand, and it's found here. You see, John had just finished writing that, yes, we all have sinned, and, yes, we all <u>HAVE</u> sin, which is that sin nature that we've all been born with. But, then he says that the things that he was writing were written <u>SO THAT WE DON'T SIN</u>! Can you understand what John was saying? He was simply telling us that we don't have to commit sin! Sin is our choice! If you take a look at some of the other writers, you'll see that they all concur. Sin is our choice!

Now, we know that there was a huge uncrossable chasm between Jesus Christ and every person who has ever lived. You see, Jesus took on humanity; but He was born without sin. There's not one single person who can make that claim. However, Jesus came as our example, our pattern, and the firstborn of many who would be conformed to His image. That's what the Word says. So, tell me something: since Jesus was born sinless, and we were not, then how is it possible that we could be made into His express image? Well, it's a lot simpler than you'd think. You see, our sin nature isn't what will keep us from that; rather, it's our propensity to commit sin. Again: sin is our choice. According to John, as well as others, we don't have to commit sin. But we've heard so often that we're just human, that we're just "sinners saved by grace", and any number of other things, that we've been trained to think that sin is inevitable. As a matter of fact, out of those four verses of Scripture in John, what's the only one we ever hear? It's the ninth verse: *"If we confess our sins, he is faithful and just to forgive us our sins, and to cleanse us from all unrighteousness"*. The Father, however, is searching for those who have the audacity to accept the fact that He can take us beyond the traditions.

Don't you understand that "the mark" is to be as Jesus was when He walked the earth some two thousand years ago?! Why else would He have endued us with the infilling of the Holy Spirit? It was to give us the *"power to become the sons of God" (John 1:12)*. No: that doesn't mean simply to be saved from our sins. It means just exactly what the Father has been trying to tell His people all along; and, that is, He's going to raise up a company of people in the EXACT LIKENESS of His firstborn Son, Jesus Christ. And, exactly as He was perfect, they'll be perfect. Not almost, not pretty near, but EXACTLY like Him. That's the goal, the mark: to be exactly like Jesus, in all of His earthly perfection.

The Prize.

So, what, then, is the prize? To understand this, you need to again consider the following portion of Scripture.

> *For whom he did foreknow, he also did predestinate to be conformed to the image of his Son, that he might be the firstborn among many brethren. (Romans 8:29)*

There's something that we don't read there; namely, "in the earth". When Paul wrote that, he didn't say that we were to be *"conformed to the image of his Son"* in the earth. In other words, God hasn't made that distinction. You see, there will be a company of people who will be conformed to the image of Jesus Christ as He was when He walked the earth, which is the mark. But, then, out of that company of people will come forth an election, a chosen group, who will be conformed to His image AS HE IS RIGHT NOW!

That's the prize!

Can you believe for the impossible? Can you believe that the Father is capable of ALL things, and that His promises and purposes go far beyond our thoughts? Can you understand that it's been the enemy's intent to keep God's people from pressing into the highest purposes of God; and he's done that by causing them to think that what the Father has promised is not what He actually meant?

DON'T LIMIT THE HOLY ONE OF ISRAEL!

Jesus Christ IS the Head of the body. IS the Head; present tense, as He is now. That means that the body HAS to be brought to the SAME level as Jesus. So, tell me: suppose the body is raised to the same spiritual level as Jesus, but not in any other way? Is that a perfect body? Not hardly. How about in any other aspect? Unless the body of Christ is raised into the EXACT SAME PLACE in every way as Jesus is now, the body will be incomplete and imperfect.

The Spirit itself beareth witness with our spirit, that we are the children of God:

And if children, then heirs; heirs of God, ***and joint-heirs with Christ; if so be that we suffer with him, that we may be also glorified together****.* *(Romans 8:16 and 17)*

JOINT-heirs! Not heirs of what's left, or of a lesser place. Heirs of what Jesus has received right now! It means that there will be a company of people who will be brought into the EXACT SAME PLACE as Jesus, in EVERY aspect, so that there will be a perfected Man, with a body that will be in perfect union with the Head. Take a look at another portion of Scripture.

Behold, what manner of love the Father hath bestowed upon us, that we should be called the sons of God: therefore the world knoweth us not, because it knew him not.

Beloved, now are we the sons of God, and it doth not yet appear what we shall be: but we know that, ***when he shall appear, we shall be like him; for we shall see him AS HE IS****.* *(1 John 3:1 and 2)*

There are a couple of things that you need to recognize here. Paul said that we ARE the sons of God right now. We HAVE been made sons by our adoption into His body through salvation. But we still haven't become what He drew us to Himself for. We haven't gotten there yet; but it's coming. However, the point that I want you to see, according to Paul, is that, when Jesus appears, there will be a company of sons who will be just like Him! Not almost like Him, and not somewhat like Him, but exactly like Him. And that will be *"when He shall appear"*. Don't you see that, when Paul was writing this, Jesus was glorified, sitting at the Father's right hand, in all of His glory? Now, Paul knew that he wouldn't be alive when Jesus appeared; but he knew that there WOULD be a company of people who would see that day. And it's THAT company of sons who *"shall be like Him . . . as He IS"*. As a matter of fact, Paul wrote about them in another place.

> *Behold, I shew you a mystery; We shall not all sleep,* ***but we shall all be changed,***
>
> ***In a moment, in the twinkling of an eye, at the last trump****: for the trumpet shall sound, and the dead shall be raised incorruptible, and we shall be changed. (1 Corinthians 15:51 and 52)*

In essence, when the glorified Jesus returns at the end of the time of tribulation, to establish His Father's Kingdom upon the earth, there will be a company of sons who will be alive, and who, having attained the perfection that He had attained when He had walked the earth, will, in the twinkling of an eye, be changed into His likeness as He will be at that time.

Now, before you start thinking that what I'm saying is that Jesus will be lowered to man's level, or that I'm suggesting that we'll gain the glory that belongs to Jesus only, let me set the record straight. ALL glory and ALL honor belongs ONLY to God; the Father, the Son, and the Holy Spirit. Remember: Jesus ONLY is the

Head, and He ONLY deserves that place of worship and honor and glory throughout the eternal ages of ages. True: Jesus is the firstborn among many brethren, but we need to recognize that the Father, in no uncertain terms, has told us that Jesus is the eternal Word, and the only One Whom HE begot (John 1:14).

So, no matter what the Father brings us to, we need to understand that Jesus Christ Himself IS the Mark and the Prize.

Jesus Christ is our goal.

<><><><><><><><><><><><><>

The point that I'm trying to make here is that, again: not every single promise in the Word of God is to every single believer; and that goes for Romans 8:29, as well. The Lord decides which promises He'll grant to each of His people, and it has nothing to do with what we want.

So, as I said, there will be a company of people who have been predestinated to be conformed to the image of Jesus Christ from before the foundation of the world. And, actually, there's not a person, dead or alive, who have any idea who they'll be. And, when the Word says, *"conformed to the image of his Son"*, it means exactly that. It doesn't mean coming close, or almost; but it means completely. It means that this company of people will attain to the exact same level spiritually, and possess the exact same attributes, and have the exact same abilities and nature, that Jesus Christ had when He walked this earth. Remember: Jesus is called the Head of the Body. Consequently, if there is any difference between the Head and the Body in ANY point, then the promise of *"a glorious church, not having spot, or wrinkle, or any such thing" (Ephesians 5:27)* becomes impotent! And we know that this promise of a glorious church is for what is to come, simply by looking at the fact that the church of the past two thousand years, and the church of today, is phenomenally schismatic!

Far too many in Christianity focus upon Jesus in primarily one point: sacrifice. The vast majority believe that the entire reason that Jesus was manifested was to be the perfect sacrifice, a substitute for us, so that He could pay the penalty for our sins; and, by doing so, make it possible for us to be reconciled to the Father, and, therefore, partakers of eternal life in glory.

That, however, is only part of it.

Not only was His sacrifice in death so critical to us, but His sacrifice in life was, too.

You see, Jesus came, not only as a substitutionary sacrifice, but as an example, as well. As the firstborn Son, He was the perfect example of what a perfect son will be. Consequently, everything that He did, and everything that He said, was to be a pattern for those who came after Him, and are called to be like Him. Take a look at a few points that emphasize what I'm talking about.

- His birth was in obscurity, recognized only by a few who were considered outcasts; and the birth of this company of people will be the same: unrecognized by the vast majority, but understood by a few.

- The enemy tried unsuccessfully to destroy Him from the very beginning; but He was protected by the Father; and those who are called to be like Him have been under divine protection for their entire lives.

- When He was a child, He received a glimpse into the things that were permitted to go on in the temple, which God had never ordained, but which the people considered to be normal; and those who are called to be like Him have been allowed to recognize the errors in the church, which far too many Christians consider to be totally acceptable.

- Jesus was born of the Spirit of God, but He HAD to receive a second anointing, which was the fulness of the Spirit, if He was to fulfill what He had been sent to do; and those who have been called have been birthed into the body of Christ by the Spirit of God; but they have to await a second anointing of the fulness of the Spirit, as well.

- Jesus experienced a time of popularity with the people, which gradually changed during His ministry, when He began to reveal that entrance into the Kingdom required the sacrifice of everything; and those who will come to be like Him will experience the same thing, and for the same reasons.

- The religious crowd always hated Jesus, because He was a threat to their way of life, and to their sway over the people, and He revealed the truth about them openly; and those who will be like Him will follow in His footsteps.

- Though He was born of the Spirit, and was declared by the Father to be His Son, still, He spent His life learning how to become the Son that He had been called to be; and those who are called to be God's chosen sons have already been declared to be those sons, yet they'll spend their entire lives learning to attain to that.

- And, just as Jesus willingly gave His entire life for those who hated Him, so will it be with those who are called to be sons in His image.

In other words, though there are multitudes who believe that Jesus is the Son of God, as well as God Himself, and though they believe that He came to pay the penalty for our sins, and though they believe that He is worthy of all praise and worship, and all rightly so, yet, far too few believe that He came to be an example of what we can become. They believe that there's a gulf between us and the perfection which Jesus attained, which we'll never be able to cross, simply because of who we are, and who He is. But, know this: the Father has made that way possible through the manifestation of Jesus as a man. No: there's absolutely no way that we can get there without the Holy Spirit. But, WITH the Holy Spirit, it's absolutely possible!

Don't let man's doubt and unbelief stop you from pressing *"toward the mark for the prize of the high calling of God in Christ Jesus" (Philippians 3:14).*

The Prism

What I've been trying to bring out in the previous chapter is the fact that the life and death of Jesus is the best example for us to follow in our quest to become a son of God. But I'm not saying that we should just copy what He did and said, as much as allowing the Holy Spirit within us to change our hearts and minds, so that we walk in obedience to the Father. In essence, one of the things that set Jesus the man apart from the rest of us is the fact that He walked in TOTAL obedience to the Father, no matter what it looked like to those who were around Him. And, all throughout the history of man, the Father has been looking for those who are of the same mind.

Now, something that stood out to me is that the Lord tells us what He requires of us, but then He gives us what we need to fulfill what He requires of us. It can be seen all throughout His Word, as well as the fact that many of us have experienced it firsthand. Thus, there's something that I want to show you concerning something that you may not have thought about.

> *Blessed are the poor in spirit: for theirs is the kingdom of heaven.*
>
> *Blessed are they that mourn: for they shall be comforted.*
>
> *Blessed are the meek: for they shall inherit the earth.*
>
> *Blessed are they which do hunger and thirst after righteousness: for they shall be filled.*
>
> *Blessed are the merciful: for they shall obtain mercy.*
>
> *Blessed are the pure in heart: for*

they shall see God.

Blessed are the peacemakers: for they shall be called the children of God.

Blessed are they which are persecuted for righteousness' sake: for theirs is the kingdom of heaven.

Blessed are ye, when men shall revile you, and persecute you, and say all manner of evil against you falsely, for my sake.

Rejoice, and be exceeding glad: for great is your reward in heaven: for so persecuted they the prophets which were before you. (Matthew 5:3 to 12)

But the fruit of the Spirit is love, joy, peace, longsuffering, gentleness, goodness, faith,

Meekness, temperance: against such there is no law. (Galatians 5:22 and 23)

What I want to bring out with these two portions of Scripture is something that you may not have recognized. You see, Galatians brings out the fruit which we should be allowing the Holy Spirit to cultivate within us; while Matthew brings out the natural outcome of the presence of the fruit in our lives. The only way that we'll be able to experience what we read about in Matthew will be through the fruit of the Spirit. And, yet, the way that we'll be able to experience the fruit of the Spirit will be through what we read about in Matthew. Thus, what I'm saying is that the two portions of Scripture are interrelated and interdependent.

Many of the points that are written in what is

called the Beatitudes in Matthew can be associated in a variety of orders with those in Galatians, and vice-versa. But, because of what the Lord has shown me, I'll be bringing them both out in the order in which we read them in the Word. After all, Jesus spoke, and Paul wrote, what the Holy Spirit gave them; and every single thing about those words were inspired, including the order in which they were given.

There's one more thing that I want to say, before I get into what I'm going to get into. I began writing this by speaking about spectroscopy, and, in particular, the Fraunhofer lines. I began in that way, because I want to show you something here. Every element in nature has a chemical signature, a "fingerprint", if you will, that makes it readily recognizable to the trained eye. Thus, for example, as light comes from a distant star or galaxy, and passes through a spectroscope, it's signature is the various lines that appear. Conversely, there are also absorption lines, which are denoted by the dark, Fraunhofer lines, where light has been absorbed. These two together determine which element or elements are present.

The reason that I've brought this out here is to say that we all have a spiritual fingerprint. Every one of us emits varying amounts and types of light, as well as Fraunhofer lines. To put it simply, we can either emit the light of the Lord's Spirit, or we can emit the Fraunhofer lines of our own spirit. And, just as physicists can determine what elements are present by the light that passes through a spectroscope, so, too, people are able to know us by the light that we do or don't emit. Far too often, we put forth a limited amount of the light of the Lord's Spirit, mixed with the Fraunhofer lines of our own spirit, which comes from absorbing the Spirit before He ever has an opportunity to be seen. And, one of the tragic things is that the unregenerate are quicker to see the truth than those who claim that they're believers. Thus, this failure on our part to show forth the light of the Lord as often as we do is one of the primary reasons that so many unregenerate are still unregenerate.

With that said, I want to explain some of the dispersions of the prism of God.

Love, And The Poor In Spirit.

But the fruit of the Spirit is love,

Blessed are the poor in spirit: for theirs is the kingdom of heaven.

There's something that both of these have in common; and both of these are so vital to our entire walk with the Lord, that He's assured that they come first. You see, without either one of these, everything else that follows will ultimately collapse.

First: love. Paul wrote:

> *Though I speak with the tongues of men and of angels, and have not charity, I am become as sounding brass, or a tinkling cymbal.*
>
> *And though I have the gift of prophecy, and understand all mysteries, and all knowledge; and though I have all faith, so that I could remove mountains, and have not charity, I am nothing.*
>
> *And though I bestow all my goods to feed the poor, and though I give my body to be burned, and have not charity,*

it profiteth me nothing. (1 Corinthians 13:1 to 3)

There have been so many preachers and teachers who have tried to explain this concept of charity, of sacrificial love; but, there's one thing they all have in common; namely, how can any finite, imperfect human do justice to that kind of love that comes only from an infinite, perfect, loving God, even with the anointing of the Holy Spirit? Believers have become so accustomed to hearing *"God so loved the world, that he gave his only begotten Son"*, that the real import of it seems to have become muddled! If I'm wrong, then explain how so many of God's people can be so wrapped up in their own things, instead of in the things of the Lord, Who gave all for us! Or, how can we profess to be a follower of the Lord Jesus on the one hand, but then get offended with, or, worse, offend, one for whom Jesus gave His life?!

Paul was a preacher of righteousness, and he brought forth what the Lord had given him to bring forth. There was a time, however, when he came to the realization that he could do all that the Lord gave him to do; but, if he didn't do it with and through the love of the Lord, he wouldn't accomplish what he needed to accomplish. Every spiritual victory would be a hollow one, and limited. You see, God is love; and everything that He does is prompted by love. Therefore, everything that the Holy Spirit is allowed to do through us has love at its core. It may sometimes appear to be harsh, but its intent is to bring life and hope and love into being. Consequently, if what we say or do doesn't have love at its core, then it means that we're speaking or acting out of our own spirit; and the eternal effects of that can be much different than we've hoped for.

Now, we may think that we pretty much know what the Lord means by love; but, do we? Can we really fathom the kind of love that the Father has for us?! We can think that we do, and we can try to explain it; but, in actuality, there's no possible way that we, in ourselves, and even with the anointing of the Spirit, can even remotely do it justice. After all, the love that the Father has is an infinite and absolutely perfect love; while the best of us are finite and far from perfect. As a matter of fact, we can begin to catch a glimpse of the love that He has; but it defies our understanding to realize that He doesn't just have love, but that He IS love. You see, we look at love as something that you feel or do, but not as something that someone is. However, the closest to explaining this is what the Holy Spirit wrote through Paul.

> *Love is patient, love is kind and is not jealous; love does not brag and is not arrogant, does not act unbecomingly; it does not seek its own, is not provoked, does not take into account a wrong suffered, does not rejoice in unrighteousness, but rejoices with the truth; bears all things, believes all things, hopes all things, endures all things. Love never fails. (1 Corinthians 13:4 to 8)*

If you notice, there's not a statement in that portion of Scripture that speaks of love being conditional. In other words, the love of God does not depend upon whether we're worthy of it, and the love of God is not a sometime thing. It IS patient, it IS kind, and so forth. It is all of those things; and NEVER do we read that it is all of those things, EXCEPT for times such as this or that. Rather, we read that God's love *"NEVER fails"*. Man's love, for the most part, fails somewhere along the line. So, when we speak of loving others, we aren't speaking about extending OUR love to them, but about allowing the Lord to extend HIS unconditional and perfect love through us to them. There's a stipulation to this, though. There's something that we always need to keep in mind in everything that we do, and in everything that we say; and it's the reason that it was the first thing that Jesus spoke to the multitudes who were gathered upon that mountain.

We always need to remember that we're ALL *"poor in spirit"*.

When we truly recognize that, then we won't balk at who the Lord sends us to, nor where He sends us; for we'll understand that there will be needs that He'll want to meet through us.

But, it goes even further than that. Think about the events surrounding the time when Jesus spoke the Beatitudes. As an aside, we have to understand that everything that Jesus taught were instructions for becoming the same kind of a son that He was; and we have to also remember that Jesus was God in the flesh. Thus, there was another time when the same thing occurred. So, first: take a look at the two accounts that I'm talking about.

> *And seeing the multitudes, he went up into a mountain: and when he was set, his disciples came unto him:*
>
> *And he opened his mouth, and taught them, saying,*
>
> *Blessed are the poor in spirit: for theirs is the kingdom of heaven. (Matthew 5:1 and 3)*

And it came to pass on the third day in the morning, that there were thunders and lightnings, and a thick cloud upon the mount, and the voice of the trumpet exceeding loud; so that all the people that was in the camp trembled.

And Moses brought forth the people out of the camp to meet with God; and they stood at the nether part of the mount.

And mount Sinai was altogether on a smoke, because the Lord descended upon it in fire: and the smoke thereof ascended as the smoke of a furnace, and the whole mount quaked greatly . . .

. . . And God spake all these words, saying,

I am the Lord thy God, which have brought thee out of the land of Egypt, out of the house of bondage.

Thou shalt have no other gods before me. (Exodus 19:16 to 19, 20:1 to 3)

Can you see the relationship between the two? Now, remember: Jesus was called Immanuel, which means, *"God with us"*. In other words, Jesus was God incarnate. The reason that I'm saying that is to show you just exactly how the event with Moses foreshadowed the event with Jesus. So, to do this, I want to compare the two.

- When God came down upon the top of mount Sinai, the name and the location are still undetermined; and, when Jesus set Himself on the top of the mountain, its location was undetermined in the Gospel.

- When God began to speak to the Israelites, it was the Word of God speaking; and when Jesus spoke to the people, it was the Word of God speaking.

- When God came down on the top of Sinai, it was with visible smoke and fire; and when Jesus set Himself on the top of the mountain, it was with the invisible fire of the Holy Spirit.

- When God spoke to the Israelites from the top of Sinai, He began to instruct them concerning what He required from them, if they were to be His people; and when Jesus taught the people, it was to instruct them concerning what God required of them if they wanted to follow Him.

- When God spoke to the Israelites, it was to give them His natural law of sacrifices; and when Jesus taught the people, it was to give them the new law of love.

- When God spoke to the people, the first six commandments focused on loving and honoring God, while the second six focused on loving and honoring our neighbor; and when Jesus taught the people, it was to give them the same commandments, but just narrowed down to two:

> *Jesus said unto him, Thou shalt love the Lord thy God with all thy heart, and with all thy soul, and with all thy mind.*
>
> *This is the first and great com-*

mandment.

And the second is like unto it, Thou shalt love thy neighbour as thyself.

On these two commandments hang all the law and the prophets. (Matthew 22:37 to 40)

There's a reason that God, on mount Sinai, started the commandments the way He did; and that Jesus, on the mount, started the Beatitudes the way He did; and that He spoke of the two greatest commandments the way He did. You see, these three give us a glimpse into what it takes to become a son, exactly the way Jesus was a Son. Everything else hangs on these; and they're all interrelated. And, the only way that we'll be able to attain to sonship is to recognize that we're absolutely poor in spirit. If we have the least bit of an idea that we have what we need spiritually within us, then we'll look to ourselves at that point; and God will be forced to take a back seat. Now, I'm not talking about just at the beginning of our walk. Rather, if we <u>EVER</u> get to that point, we'll find ourselves teetering on the edge of losing sight of the Lord, and replacing Him with ourselves! We can see that in John's letter to the Laodiceans.

Because thou sayest, I am rich, and increased with goods, and have need of nothing; and knowest not that thou art wretched, and miserable, and poor, and blind, and naked: (Revelation 3:17)

There's something else that I want to point out here. We know what Jesus spoke to the multitudes, and the words that He used. But, what He said has its roots much further back. You see, the idea of the poor in spirit is speaking about humility, and the necessity of it in our walk with Him. That, then, takes us to a few portions of Scripture. And, keep in mind that there's a relationship amongst them, which I'll show you in a short bit. So, consider the following.

> *Pride goeth before destruction, and an haughty spirit before a fall.*
>
> *Better it is to be of an humble spirit with the lowly, than to divide the spoil with the proud. (Proverbs 16:18 and 19)*

> *By humility and the fear of the Lord are riches, and honour, and life. (Proverbs 22:4)*

> *An angry man stirreth up strife, and a furious man aboundeth in transgression.*
>
> *A man's pride shall bring him low: but honour shall uphold the humble in spirit. (Proverbs 29:22 and 23)*

> *For thus saith the high and lofty One that inhabiteth eternity, whose name is Holy; I dwell in the high and holy place, with him also that is of a contrite and humble spirit, to revive the spirit of the humble, and to revive the heart of the contrite ones. (Isaiah 57:15)*

So, to look at the first two portions of Scripture, I want to recount something that occurred centuries ago. There was a time when the Lord called Gideon to lead the children of Israel to a victory over the Midianites. Gideon raised an army of 32,000 men, and prepared to do battle with their enemy. However, the Lord told him that 32,000 were far too many for His purposes; and, by the time He finished, He ultimately whittled the army down to 300. Now, it wasn't that the Midianites were a weak enemy. Actually, they were quite a formidable one, and had kept Israel in subjection for quite some time. But, the Lord explained it very clearly.

> *The people that are with thee are too many for me to give the Midianites into their hands, lest Israel vaunt themselves against me, saying, Mine own hand hath saved me. (Judges 7:2)*

So, in this, there are a number of things that the Lord wants us to understand about walking with Him, and about becoming a son.

First: pride and haughtiness will give us the delusion that we can be independent. We face so many things during the course of the day; and we usually don't give much of it a second thought, because they're things that we do regularly. But, we need to realize that, if it wasn't for the Lord in EVERY situation, we'd fall flat on our face every time. HE enables us to breathe, to think, to live. If it wasn't for Him, our lives would quickly come to an abrupt end.

That, then, takes us to the second point: we need to know that it's impossible for us to face the things we go through alone. We really don't have what it takes when we come face to face with life at its harshest. So, humility leaves us no other alternative than to turn to the Lord; and that enables us to do things that we never thought we'd be able to do.

The third point that I want to bring out here is

that there's something that we need, not to recognize, but to accept: the proud WILL acquire riches and favor and fame. There's nothing that we can do about it, simply because this is their world right now, and their world honors them. Those will, however, be temporal gains; and they'll actually accomplish a purpose. Because the proud determine their greatness and favor by their gain and prosperity, then it separates between them and the humble, between the self-seekers and the God-seekers, between the wheat and the tares. That's why God told us:

> *Fret not thyself because of evildoers, neither be thou envious against the workers of iniquity.*
>
> *For they shall soon be cut down like the grass, and wither as the green herb. (Psalm 37:1 and 2)*

You see, according to Proverbs 22:4 that I mentioned, the true, eternal riches and honor and life come through humility and the fear of the Lord.

And fourth: don't question His ways. Gideon originally had no idea that the Lord was going to cut his army of 32,000 down to 300. As a matter of fact, all throughout the Word of God, we read of similar things, where He required His true followers to do things that didn't seem to make sense to the natural mind. But He tells us, in no uncertain terms:

> *For my thoughts are not your thoughts, neither are your ways my ways, saith the Lord.*
>
> *For as the heavens are higher than the earth, so are my ways higher than*

your ways, and my thoughts than your thoughts. (Isaiah 55:8 and 9)

That means that, if we want to attain to being a son of God in the image of His firstborn Son, Jesus, then we need to follow His ways, without question.

So, as you may have seen, the first two portions of Scripture in Proverbs that I mentioned had a direct relationship with each other. Consequently, I can see the same thing with the last two that I mentioned. At the same time, there's a relationship in the way the first two are worded, and then the second two. Thus, the four are interrelated with each other, as well as with Matthew 5:3. And, in the portion from Proverbs 29, we can see something that can also be seen in what Paul wrote.

Your glorying is not good. Know ye not that a little leaven leaveneth the whole lump? (1 Corinthians 5:6)

In that instance, it was the fact that the Corinthians were actually puffed up concerning something that was being done openly amongst them. However, that, and the instruction in Proverbs, both address the same concept. You see, the most common leaven that was used was a lump of old dough that was in a high state of fermentation. The resulting gas from fermentation entered the dough, and caused it to rise. But, again: that's old dough, not fresh. Another way of looking at it is that it was corrupted dough that leavened the good dough. That's why the Lord never allowed any leaven in His sacrifices.

So, we have a choice. It's either humility, or pride; humility, or strife; humility, or transgression; humility, or destruction. Those who <u>CHOOSE</u> humility, who CHOOSE to recognize and confess that they're poor in spirit, will *"dwell in the high and holy place"* with Him Who inhabits eternity! Jesus told us that those who are poor in spirit will inherit the kingdom of heaven; and He intentionally began all of His instruction to the people with that, simply because that's the cornerstone of becoming a son in His likeness.

Joy, And They That Mourn.

Of all the aspects that I'm going to bring out, "joy" and "mourning" seem to be the most in direct opposition to each other. But, as I've said before, the Word of God doesn't contradict itself in any point. So, actually, if you think about it: joy and mourning are perfect complements to each other, and are two aspects of the Spirit that are integral parts of the true believer's life.

When I considered "joy" and "mourning", I took a look at all of the Scriptures in the Word where they could be found, including the variations of the words. Thus, in both the Old and New Testaments, there were (124) Scriptures which spoke of mourning, while there were (179) which spoke of joy. What I found interesting was the fact that there were almost as many Scriptures referring to joy in the Old Testament alone (119) as there were references to mourning in the entire Word of God. Then again, there were (13) references to mourning in the New Testament, while there were (60) speaking of joy. Thus, there's something that the Lord wants His people to understand: joy and mourning both have a place in our lives, and both are intricately related, so that we can be brought into the image of Jesus Christ. If we give precedence to either one over the other, our walk in Him will be hampered.

I want to start here by taking a look at the aspect

of mourning; and I want to clarify something. As with pretty much everything, we can function according to the Spirit, or we can function according to the flesh. So, there are those who mourn according to the Spirit of the Lord, such as Jeremiah, Ezekiel, Hosea, and Jesus outside of Jerusalem. But, then, there are those who mourn through tradition, such as the Pharisees. What it boils down to is the fact that mourning is allowing the Spirit to use us to intercede for the conditions which exist in the secular and religious worlds right now. Thus, we can try to do that in ourselves; but, as we read:

> *Likewise the Spirit also helpeth our infirmities: for we know not what we should pray for as we ought: but the Spirit itself maketh intercession for us with groanings which cannot be uttered. (Romans 8:26)*

Now, don't get me wrong. The Lord will honor our attempts to mourn, even if we do so in the flesh. But our ministrations in the flesh, when we believe that we're fulfilling His requirements, are a sign of immaturity. The Lord, however, expects His people to grow up; and that means that He expects us to learn how to walk in the Spirit. As an aside, maturity in the Spirit simply means that we walk more like Jesus did than like we have our entire lives. So, He'll honor our attempts to mourn, when done in the flesh; but His acceptance of that is ultimately limited.

There's another aspect of mourning that we need to understand; and it's far more self-directed. What I'm talking about is the fact that we need to look at ourselves, before we ever look at others. When Jesus taught the people from the mount, He told them something that went against everything that they had been accustomed to hearing from the religious hierarchy that ruled over them in the seat of Moses.

> *Judge not, that ye be not judged.*
>
> *For with what judgment ye judge, ye shall be judged: and with what measure ye mete, it shall be measured to you again.*
>
> *And why beholdest thou the mote that is in thy brother's eye, but considerest not the beam that is in thine own eye?*
>
> *Or how wilt thou say to thy brother, Let me pull out the mote out of thine eye; and, behold, a beam is in thine own eye?*
>
> *Thou hypocrite, first cast out the beam out of thine own eye; and then shalt thou see clearly to cast out the mote out of thy brother's eye. (Matthew 7:1 to 5)*

Many of the Pharisees were noted for trying to enforce the law of Moses, as well as all the multitude of other laws that they formulated, while finding some self-promulgated "loopholes" that conveniently "excluded" them from having to obey those very same laws. They would judge, while ignoring what was in themselves that the Lord was judging. As a matter of fact, the number one reason for people staying away from churches is because of what they perceive as hypocrisy in the ministry and in the people. Those who come to that place don't seem to understand that, while they get upset at the judgmental spirit in many churches, they're actually lumping all believers into one category, and passing judgment upon them; which, therefore, makes them as judgmental as those whom they're decrying. Our primary place is not to make other people to follow the Lord faithfully, but to allow the Holy Spirit to bring to our knowledge those things that He wants us to work on with Him, so that He can cleanse us, and bring us into the likeness of Jesus Christ. And, if we're truly serious with Him, and with attaining to Jesus, then, when those things that are displeasing to the Lord are revealed to us, our reaction WILL be one of mourning, and, hopefully, true repentance. Yes, the Lord may use us to reveal things to others that are displeasing to Him; but those times should be ONLY through Him, NOT through our zeal. Now, take a look at the following portion of Scripture.

> *And because iniquity shall abound, the love of many shall wax cold. (Matthew 24:12)*

Do you know what mourning really is? Simply: it's the manifestation of the love of the Lord for those who are standing against Him, or who are straying from Him, and who are walking in their own spirit. We could very easily choose to ignore them, or to allow them to receive what they rightly deserve. But, the bottom line is: if we really desire to become like Jesus, then we'll truly love as He loved. Far too many, including more and more believers, are adopting a negative attitude toward those who disagree with them. Consequently, it's driving nonbelievers away from a possible relationship with Jesus. Remember: hypocrisy is the number one thing that people claim is turning them off to Christianity; and there's nothing more hypocritical than hearing believers speaking about loving as the Lord loved, but then berating others. The Lord mourns for that, as well as the numerous other conditions that exist in the world today; and that should prompt us to mourn for those, as well.

There's a definite manifestation because of this; namely: joy. Now, I'm not talking about the smiley, happy, party atmosphere that permeates far too many churches today, especially in America. Rather, I'm talking about the kind of joy that arises in the midst of heartaches and trouble; the joy that defies our own, and everyone else's, understanding; because, when we should be depressed and weeping, or angry and lashing out, we're instead at complete peace. As a matter of fact, it goes beyond just peace, to a joy that impacts those with whom we come into contact. You see, because of our being willing to allow ourselves to endure the mourning of the Spirit for the condition of the church and of the world, which tends to result in spiritual and physical exhaustion, then the Lord gives us that special anointing of joy, that replenishes all of that, and much, much more! Look at just a few places in the Word where we read that; and consider who wrote those words, and what they had gone through during their lives.

> *I cried to thee, O Lord; and unto the Lord I made supplication.*
>
> *What profit is there in my blood, when I go down to the pit? Shall the dust praise thee? shall it declare thy truth?*
>
> *Hear, O Lord, and have mercy upon me; Lord, be thou my helper.*
>
> *Thou hast turned for me my mourning into dancing: thou hast put off my sackcloth, and girded me with gladness;*
>
> *To the end that my glory may sing*

praise to thee, and not be silent, O Lord my God, I will give thanks unto thee for ever. (Psalm 30:8 to 12)

The Spirit of the Lord God is upon me; because the Lord hath anointed me to preach good tidings unto the meek; he hath sent me to bind up the brokenhearted, to proclaim liberty to the captives, and the opening of the prison to them that are bound;

To proclaim the acceptable year of the Lord, and the day of vengeance of our God; to comfort all that mourn;

To appoint unto them that mourn in Zion, to give unto them beauty for ashes, the oil of joy for mourning, the garment of praise for the spirit of heaviness; that they might be called trees of righteousness, the planting of the Lord, that he might be glorified. (Isaiah 61:1 to 3)

Hear the word of the Lord, O ye nations, and declare it in the isles afar off, and say, He that scattered Israel will gather him, and keep him, as a shepherd doth his flock.

For the Lord hath redeemed Jacob, and ransomed him from the hand of him that was stronger than he.

Therefore they shall come and sing in the height of Zion, and shall flow together to the goodness of the Lord, for wheat, and for wine, and for oil, and for the young of the flock and of the herd:

and their soul shall be as a watered garden; and they shall not sorrow any more at all.

Then shall the virgin rejoice in the dance, both young men and old together: for I will turn their mourning into joy, and will comfort them, and make them rejoice from their sorrow.

And I will satiate the soul of the priests with fatness, and my people shall be satisfied with my goodness, saith the Lord. (Jeremiah 31:10 to 14)

Now Jesus knew that they were desirous to ask him, and said unto them, Do ye enquire among yourselves of that I said, A little while, and ye shall not see me: and again, a little while, and ye shall see me?

Verily, verily, I say unto you, That ye shall weep and lament, but the world shall rejoice: and ye shall be sorrowful, but your sorrow shall be turned into joy.

A woman when she is in travail hath sorrow, because her hour is come: but as soon as she is delivered of the child, she remembereth no more the anguish, for joy that a man is born into the world.

And ye now therefore have sorrow: but I will see you again, and your heart shall rejoice, and your joy no man taketh from you. (John 16:19 to 22)

Though these were just a few portions of Scripture which look at joy and mourning, there's one thing that they all have in common. Each one of them speaks of joy that is focused upon the Lord, and upon His Kingdom. You see, there are any number of things that bring joy to people. Almost everyone can think of one or more times when they felt joy in their lives. But, in most cases, it's a physical, natural, relatively short-lived joy, bordering more upon happiness than true joy. The reason for that lies in the fact that, no matter how good we feel when the joy comes from a natural situation, it still fails to attain to the true joy that comes from the Lord.

This, then, is what many in the church, especially in this country, miss. There seems to be such an emphasis on "the joy of the Lord", that other critical things are overlooked or ignored. Now, I'm not saying that the joy that the Lord gives is not important; but, when the focus is almost exclusively upon that, then it's an imbalanced spiritual walk. There's something else about the joy of the Lord that we'll find in so many churches; and, that is, it could be called "the happiness of the Lord". In other words, the true joy of the Lord isn't something that is worked up by a whole lot of dancing and shouting and what could be called a party-like atmosphere. Know this: though the joy that the Lord gives isn't worked up by outward expressions, such as dancing and shouting, dancing and shouting can be expressions of His joy. So, we can't pass judgment upon those who are expressing their feelings, no matter what we think.

Peace, And The Meek.

Whenever we think of "peace" and of "meekness", we tend to have a prescribed notion about each one. Ask any number of people about their definition of each, and you'll find that most, including believers, will state that "peace" means a time when all is in harmony; and that one who is "meek" is very docile, equating it with shyness. However, I want to give you something to think about that may change your ideas about what the Lord requires of His people.

To start, I want to take a look at the idea of meekness. As I said, many people, including believers, tend to look at meekness as docility and shyness. But consider the following portion of Scripture. Though what I'll be quoting is a little longer than I normally would, there are a couple of things in it that I need to bring out.

> *And Miriam and Aaron spake against Moses because of the Ethiopian woman whom he had married: for he had married an Ethiopian woman.*
>
> *And they said, Hath the Lord indeed spoken only by Moses? hath he not spoken also by us? And the Lord heard it.*
>
> *(Now the man Moses was very meek, above all the men which were upon the face of the earth.)*
>
> *And the Lord spake suddenly unto Moses, and unto Aaron, and unto Miriam, Come out ye three unto the tabernacle of the congregation. And they three came out.*
>
> *And the Lord came down in the pillar of the cloud, and stood in the door of the tabernacle, and called Aaron and Miriam: and they both came forth.*
>
> *And he said, Hear now my words: If there be a prophet among you, I the Lord will make myself known unto him in a vision, and will speak unto him in a*

dream.

My servant Moses is not so, who is faithful in all mine house.

With him will I speak mouth to mouth, even apparently, and not in dark speeches; and the similitude of the Lord shall he behold: wherefore then were ye not afraid to speak against my servant Moses?

And the anger of the Lord was kindled against them; and he departed.

And the cloud departed from off the tabernacle; and, behold, Miriam became leprous, white as snow: and Aaron looked upon Miriam, and, behold, she was leprous.

And Aaron said unto Moses, Alas, my Lord, I beseech thee, lay not the sin upon us, wherein we have done foolishly, and wherein we have sinned.

Let her not be as one dead, of whom the flesh is half consumed when he cometh out of his mother's womb.

And Moses cried unto the Lord, saying, Heal her now, O God, I beseech thee.

And the Lord said unto Moses, If her father had but spit in her face, should she not be ashamed seven days? let her be shut out from the camp seven days, and after that let her be received in again.

And Miriam was shut out from the camp seven days: and the people journeyed not till Miriam was brought in again.

> *And afterward the people removed from Hazeroth, and pitched in the wilderness of Paran. (Numbers 12)*

There are a couple of things in this that God's people need to understand.

The first thing is the fact that meekness really has very little to do with the idea of shyness; though there's some semblance of docility; but not in the sense that it's traditionally thought of. The Greek term holds the concept of our accepting the dealings of God without disputing Him, nor resisting Him. But shy? Not hardly. As a matter of fact, as we've read: *"Moses was very meek, above all the men"*. But this was the same man who stood before Pharaoh, and demanded the release of the children of Israel. He's the same one who commanded the slaughter of those Israelites who had sinned before the golden calf when he descended Mount Sinai with the tables of the law, seen in Exodus chapter 32. He's the same one who gave God an ultimatum concerning His leading the children of Israel, seen in Exodus chapter 33. And he's the same one who spoke God's judgment upon Korah and Dathan, Abiram and On, when the ground opened up, and destroyed all of the rebels, seen in Numbers chapter 16.

What I'm saying through this is what the Lord has been trying to get us to realize; namely, we need to change our ideas about meekness. As a matter of fact, meekness takes more courage and faith than far too many believers are willing to put forth. Sadly, it's a lot easier to gripe and complain about what comes our way, than to say, *"Nevertheless not as I will, but as thou wilt" (Matthew 26:39)*, and truly mean it. Easy? No! But if we want to have a place in the Lord's Kingdom, it's something that He requires of us.

The second thing has to do with when Miriam was struck with leprosy because of her willingly speaking against Moses. Aaron pleaded with Moses to intercede for her healing, and Moses then asked the Lord to heal her. But the instant healing never came. This was the man whom the Lord spoke with face to face, and who had special favor with Him. Aaron knew that, and had seen plenty of times when Moses received whatever he asked for from God. But, again, the instant healing never came. True: He had commanded that, after seven days, she would be healed; but nothing would cause Him to abrogate that.

There are a whole lot of believers who stand by the fact that the sacrifice of Jesus on the cross included the provision for healing. I want to stress the point that healing through the sacrifice of Jesus is a indisputable fact, no matter what anybody else thinks or says. But, there are also far too many believers who expect that the Lord's response to our prayers for healing are always yea, and amen. Part of the meekness of Moses lay in his ability to learn the lessons that the Lord taught him, no matter what they were. So, regarding his request for the healing of Miriam, God's refusal taught Moses something of which he hadn't been aware. If you notice, Moses didn't argue with the Lord, nor did he sulk and grumble. He simply accepted God's answer. And he learned that there would be times when he wouldn't receive what he asked for; at least, not in the way that he expected it.

And that's a lesson that we all need to learn.

Now, the other side of this coin that I want to look at has to do with "peace"; and there's a definite relationship between that, and "meekness". You see, there are a couple of different concepts with peace; and the two concepts seem to be diametrically opposed to each other. But, are they?

So, the start: what do we think of when we consider the term "peace"? Well, very simply, it speaks of freedom from conflict, when everything is in harmony. This is pretty much the primary idea behind it. But, where it gets a little more complicated is in determining how that peace is attained. For that, take a look at a couple of portions of Scripture.

> *And it came to pass, when the king sat in his house, and the Lord had given him rest round about from all his enemies; (2 Samuel 7:1)*

> *And he said, Go and spy where he is, that I may send and fetch him. And it was told him, saying, Behold, he is in Dothan.*
>
> *Therefore sent he thither horses, and chariots, and a great host: and they came by night, and compassed the city about.*
>
> *And when the servant of the man of God was risen early, and gone forth, behold, an host compassed the city both with horses and chariots. And his servant said unto him, Alas, my master! how shall we do?*
>
> *And he answered, Fear not: for they that be with us are more than they that be with them.*
>
> *And Elisha prayed, and said, Lord, I pray thee, open his eyes, that he may see. And the Lord opened the eyes of the young man; and he saw: and, behold, the*

mountain was full of horses and chariots of fire round about Elisha.

And when they came down to him, Elisha prayed unto the Lord, and said, Smite this people, I pray thee, with blindness. And he smote them with blindness according to the word of Elisha.

And Elisha said unto them, This is not the way, neither is this the city: follow me, and I will bring you to the man whom ye seek. But he led them to Samaria.

And it came to pass, when they were come into Samaria, that Elisha said, Lord, open the eyes of these men, that they may see. And the Lord opened their eyes, and they saw; and, behold, they were in the midst of Samaria.

And the king of Israel said unto Elisha, when he saw them, My father, shall I smite them? shall I smite them?

And he answered, Thou shalt not smite them: wouldest thou smite those whom thou hast taken captive with thy sword and with thy bow? set bread and water before them, that they may eat and drink, and go to their master.

And he prepared great provision for them: and when they had eaten and drunk, he sent them away, and they went to their master. So the bands of Syria came no more into the land of Israel. (2 Kings 6:13 to 23)

There are quite a few other portions of Scripture

that I could have brought out here, but these two should be sufficient to say what I'm going to say. In the first one, God gave David rest, or peace, from all of his enemies. Do you know how? Through warfare. And in the second one, there was peace from the bands of Syria; and that came because they experienced the power and the mercy of the Lord. The Lord, then, gives peace to His people through warfare, and He gives it to them through His power and His mercy. And there's a particular reason that He gives it.

What I'm saying, then, is that the Lord doesn't have a set way that He gives rest in our lives. And there's where the meekness comes into play. In other words, we have to be willing to learn that He <u>DOES</u> do things differently than we think and expect. Let me give you an example.

When the Lord came to deliver the children of Israel from the bondage of Egypt by the hand of Moses, they saw His judgments upon their captors, while they experienced His mercy in the land of Goshen. They also experienced His mercy upon them in their journey to the wilderness of Sinai. Consequently, when He called them forth to the mount, so that He could speak with them, they expected to hear from a God of mercy and love, as they perceived Him.

They expected mercy and grace. But, He was different; and they wouldn't accept Him.

Fifteen hundred years later, God appeared as the man Jesus, to deliver whomsoever will from the bondage of the flesh, the devil, and the world. But, because the Jews had been accustomed to seeing God as the only God, with none other beside Him, and because they were accustomed to a litany of laws and commandments, and because they failed to see that God's ultimate intentions were to redeem <u>ALL</u> of mankind, then they expected a Messiah Who ruled with an iron fist, and Who would put all of their enemies, such as Rome, under their feet.

They expected judgment, and a conquering King. But He was different; and they wouldn't accept Him.

Now, over the last twenty plus centuries, the church has preached Jesus Christ, and Him crucified, to extend mercy and grace to a lost creation. And they've been preaching about Jesus returning at the end of this age, to deliver His people from this world, and to judge those who haven't accepted Him.

They're expecting Jesus Who walked the earth to return before the time of tribulation. But He's going to be different; and they won't accept Him!

What I'm saying is wrapped up in the following portion of Scripture.

> *For my thoughts are not your thoughts, neither are your ways my ways, saith the Lord.*
>
> *For as the heavens are higher than the earth, so are my ways higher than your ways, and my thoughts than your thoughts. (Isaiah 55:8 and 9)*

So, we need to learn that God will give us rest from our enemies in any manner that He deems to be best for us; and we need to accept whatever way He chooses. That's the meekness. But, giving us rest from our enemies falls into that category spoken of in Isaiah 55; namely, that we have one idea about what being delivered from our enemies is, while the Lord sometimes has a different idea. And that's what we need to accept. Remember this that Paul wrote?

> *And lest I should be exalted above measure through the abundance of the revelations, there was given to me a thorn in the flesh, the messenger of Satan to buffet me, lest I should be exalted above measure.*
>
> *For this thing I besought the Lord thrice, that it might depart from me.*
>
> *And he said unto me, My grace is sufficient for thee: for my strength is made perfect in weakness. Most gladly therefore will I rather glory in my infirmities, that the power of Christ may rest upon me. (2 Corinthians 12:7 to 9)*

Do you realize that there are many times when the Lord doesn't deliver us from the power of our enemies in the way that we expect? But we can have rest from every one of our enemies, nonetheless. Now, that may seem to be contradictory, unless you realize that God doesn't contradict Himself. In short, we can be in the midst of all hell breaking loose in our life; but, if we've really, truly accepted that *"ALL things work together for good to them that love God, to them who are the called according to his purpose" (Romans 8:28)*, then we'll be at peace, having been delivered from the power of every one of our enemies. As long as we look to the Lord, and rest in Him, then we'll walk in the peace that He's promised.

Now, the primary reason that He wants us to bear every fruit of the Spirit is not specifically for us. Rather, His intentions are for us to extend those fruits to others. So, despite the way so many are today, He wants us to interject His Spirit into the midst of each situation. But, if we don't have the fruits of the Spirit working in our lives, then there's no way that we'll be able to extend them to others. You see, the Lord wants to feed a lost creation; and He'll only feed them with fruit. After all, He intends their food to be fruit, simply because that was what He gave for food in the garden; and all who partake of the fruit of the Spirit will live in the realm of the garden.

Longsuffering, And To Hunger And Thirst After Righteousness.

> *Hear ye therefore the parable of the sower.*
>
> *When any one heareth the word of the kingdom, and understandeth it not, then cometh the wicked one, and catcheth away that which was sown in his heart. This is he which received seed by the way side.*
>
> *But he that received the seed into stony places, the same is he that heareth the word, and anon with joy receiveth it;*
>
> *Yet hath he not root in himself, but dureth for a while: for when tribulation or persecution ariseth because of the word, by and by he is offended.*
>
> *He also that received seed among the thorns is he that heareth the word; and the care of this world, and the deceitfulness of riches, choke the word, and he becometh unfruitful.*
>
> *But he that received seed into the good ground is he that heareth the word, and understandeth it; which also beareth fruit, and bringeth forth, some an*

hundredfold, some sixty, some thirty. (Matthew 13:18 to 23)

There are a couple of things that each one of these who received the Word had in common; and it's called time and depth. But, beside that, we can see a progression of those things. Consequently, with the first recipient, the Word didn't really have an opportunity to take root, and it was lost in a relatively short time. With the second, there was some depth, which meant that it had begun to take root. Unfortunately, even though the Word was accepted joyfully, the reality of walking with the Lord became evident; and it was abandoned. The third received the Word, and they held on through the times of persecution and tribulation. But, the cares and the riches of the world overshadowed the Word, and it was ultimately lost. Finally, we see those who received the Word, and who understood it; and it took root, and thrived.

So, can you see the progression that I'm talking about? The Word never took root with the first person, simply because of a stony heart; and it was snatched away rather quickly by the enemy. The Word remained with the second one, but only for a short while; and the persecution and tribulation that accompanies it caused a change of heart. With the third, the enemy couldn't drive the Word from them through persecution and tribulation; but he was able to succeed through the cares and the riches of the world. He failed, however, when it came to the fourth one; for the understanding of the Word became grounded in them. They were able to withstand whatever came at them, and, through those things, they were able to bring forth fruit, *"some an hundredfold, some sixty, some thirty"*.

What I'm getting at is very simple: attaining the

best in God requires longsuffering and hunger. Nothing of any eternal worth comes to us in an instant. Even when it comes to salvation and the baptism in the Holy Spirit, things are different than we tend to think, because of the way they're presented by so many in the church. The receipt of the forgiveness of sins is an instantaneous thing; but salvation is a lifelong walk with the Lord. And, though the baptism in the Holy Spirit is also an instantaneous thing, it takes a lifetime to learn how to walk in the Spirit.

There is, however, something that we need to realize. If we don't *"hunger and thirst after righteousness"*, we'll never attain what He's promised. And there's something else that we need to realize in connection with this. Ever since the fall in the garden, <u>EVERY</u> person who has ever lived, and ever will live, experience that emptiness and hunger, simply because of our separation from God. But there's something more that we need to realize; and it's quite sobering. Far too few, even amongst those who claim to be followers of Jesus, really, truly, *"hunger and thirst after righteousness"*. Rather, so many are hungering and thirsting for whatever they can attain for their own personal gain. Their desire is for what this world can give them, instead of what the Lord can. And, another sobering thought is the fact that many of them have the longsuffering needed to attain those things that stand in opposition to God.

We <u>HAVE</u> to understand that the Lord allows us to *"hunger and thirst after righteousness"*; but, to attain that righteousness, He requires us to endure with longsuffering whatever He allows to come our way, so that the end result will be our attainment of that righteousness. Consider the following portions of Scripture.

And the Scripture was fulfilled

> *which saith, Abraham believed God, and it was imputed unto him for righteousness: and he was called the Friend of God. (James 2:23)*

> *Greater love hath no man than this, that a man lay down his life for his friends.*
>
> *Ye are my friends, if ye do whatsoever I command you.*
>
> *Henceforth I call you not servants; for the servant knoweth not what his Lord doeth: but I have called you friends; for all things that I have heard of my Father I have made known unto you. (John 15:13 to 15)*

That's what those who are true followers of Jesus are seeking after: to become friends of God. To be His friend means that there's an intimacy between Him and us. To be His friend means that He'll reveal His plans and purposes to us. And to be His friend means that He'll bestow that special righteousness upon us that He won't upon anyone else. Abraham had a special place with God, and His friends have that same place.

But it takes three things to get there. First: we have to desire it with all that is within us. We have to *"hunger and thirst"* after it. Second: we also have to pursue it with all that is within us; and that means being willing to endure with all longsuffering to ultimately attain that. True righteousness, and true friendship with God, takes a lifetime of cultivation. And, third: that cultivation is wrapped up in the term *"obedience"*. Jesus put it very bluntly when He told His disciples, and, by extension, us, that, if we want to be His friend, then we have to do whatever He commands us to do.

And, as an aside: how often have we heard the Scripture quoted, where Jesus said, *"Greater love hath no man than this, that a man lay down his life for his friends"*? True: Jesus was affirming that He was going to lay His life down for those whom He called friends, as well as for all mankind. But, if we seek to be called His friend, then WE have to lay OUR life down for HIM, as well as for every one for whom He laid down His life.

Gentleness, And The Merciful.

> *And even as they did not like to retain God in their knowledge, God gave them over to a reprobate mind, to do those things which are not convenient;*
>
> *Being filled with all unrighteousness, fornication, wickedness, covetousness, maliciousness; full of envy, murder, debate, deceit, malignity; whisperers,*
>
> *Backbiters, haters of God, despiteful, proud, boasters, inventors of evil things, disobedient to parents,*
>
> *Without understanding, covenantbreakers, without natural affection, implacable, unmerciful:*
>
> *Who knowing the judgment of God, that they which commit such things are worthy of death, not only do the same, but have pleasure in them that do them. (Romans 1:28 to 32)*

That was the world in Paul's day, and it's the same in the world today. If you're old enough, think how it was some fifty years ago, or even twenty years ago.

What goes on today are things that would never have entered most of our minds back then. As a matter of fact, that seems to be the universal statement that has been made by people in areas where some of these mass shootings have taken place: "We never thought that it could happen here!" More and more, people are putting walls up between themselves, and finding more and more reasons to alienate each other.

In reality, this stems from one definite source: Satan. And the reason for this is because we're in the last days. The last days of what? The last days of the kingdom of Satan upon the earth. He knows that he's quickly reaching the end of his authority, and he's ramping up his assaults upon those who are under his control, and especially upon those who have entered the Kingdom of God.

The reason I brought this out the way I did is to say something about what the Lord requires of those who are seeking to come into His likeness. You see, what people are seeking for in others is something that they don't realize comes from the Lord; and two of those things are gentleness and mercy. Again: look at what so much of the world looks like today. The two things that we see so very little of is gentleness and mercy. Rather, we see confusion, and bitterness, and anger, and every other thing that is characteristic of the enemy. Understand this: the world is looking for gentleness and mercy; but they're finding precious too little of it! And, tragically, they aren't finding it, to a great degree, where they should be able to; and that's from those who call themselves followers of the Lord! Consequently, they're turning away from Him. And, when you turn away from the Lord, there's only one other place to go!

God expects His people to bear the fruit of gentleness. He hasn't made it optional; He's made it mandatory, if we want to be a part of His Kingdom. And the result of that gentleness will be mercy. Now, by gentleness, I'm not talking about wimpiness. People tend to think of it that way, just as they tend to think of meekness along the same line. Actually, both meekness and gentleness require a strength that very few people possess, simply because they both stand in opposition to the character of so many people.

There's something else that has to be a part of this gentleness; and that's honesty. Now, I don't mean honesty in the sense of admitting when we do something wrong; but honesty in the way that Jesus was honest.

> *Jesus answered, Verily, verily, I say unto thee, Except a man be born of water and of the Spirit, he cannot enter into the kingdom of God.*
>
> *That which is born of the flesh is flesh; and that which is born of the Spirit is spirit.*
>
> *Marvel not that I said unto thee, Ye must be born again.*
>
> *The wind bloweth where it listeth, and thou hearest the sound thereof, but canst not tell whence it cometh, and whither it goeth: so is every one that is born of the Spirit.*
>
> *Nicodemus answered and said unto him, How can these things be?*
>
> *Jesus answered and said unto him, Art thou a master of Israel, and knoweth not these things? (John 3:5 to 10)*

> *Jesus answered and said unto her,*

Whosoever drinketh of this water shall thirst again:

But whosoever drinketh of the water that I shall give him shall never thirst; but the water that I shall give him shall be in him a well of water springing up into everlasting life.

The woman saith unto him, Sir, give me this water, that I thirst not, neither come hither to draw.

Jesus saith unto her, Go, call thy husband, and come hither.

The woman answered and said, I have no husband. Jesus said unto her, Thou hast well said, I have no husband:

For thou hast had five husbands; and he whom thou now hast is not thy husband: in that saidst thou truly. (John 4:13 to 18)

Did you notice the answers that Jesus gave in each of those instances? If it had been many of us in the same place, we might have told Nicodemus, "You're kidding! With all that you claim you are, and you don't know what I'm talking about?! What kind of a teacher do you call yourself?!" And, with the Samaritan woman, we might have first severely rebuked her for her living arrangements before we ever said anything about the water. Jesus, however, did nothing of the sort; yet, in a way, He did. The difference lay in the fact that, when He pointed up the fact that Nicodemus should have been, but wasn't, aware of the truths about which He was speaking, He did it so that Nicodemus didn't feel threatened. And when He revealed that He knew the truth of the situation to the Samaritan woman, she didn't feel threatened, but, rather, amazed that He knew. In other words, He addressed the truth completely honestly, but He did with a gentleness that didn't threaten His hearers. The result was that they were open to receiving His mercy that changed the situation for them, and everyone that knew them. Consequently, when we allow the fruit of gentleness to come forth, His mercy will follow.

Goodness, And The Pure In Heart.

As I was looking at these two aspects, a couple of things came to mind.

> *And, behold, one came and said unto him, Good Master, what good thing shall I do, that I may have eternal life?*
> *And he said unto him, Why callest thou me good? there is none good but one, that is, God: but if thou wilt enter into life, keep the commandments. (Matthew 19:16 and 17)*

> *The heart is deceitful above all things, and desperately wicked: who can know it?*
> *I the Lord search the heart, I try the reins, even to give every man according to his ways, and according to the fruit of his doings. (Jeremiah 17:9 and 10)*

I have something to ask you. Since Jesus responded to being called *"Good Master"* as He did, and since Jeremiah tells us about the condition of our heart, then how can we expect to have *"goodness"*, and to be *"pure in heart"*? Yet, again, these are not options for those who seek to be like Jesus.

First: when we think of Jesus, the word *"good"* seems to be perfectly descriptive of Him. But, then, why did He say what He did to being called *"Good Master"*? Well, that statement was directed at Jesus, not as Lord and Savior, but as a human teacher. Consequently, He was directing that away from Him in His humanity, by bluntly saying that *"there is none good but one, that is, God"*. He wanted His listeners to understand that, if goodness is to be found, it can be found only in God. As a matter of fact, goodness is perfect ONLY in God, and everything else is in limited perfection of varying degrees. He knew that, if He allowed the claim of *"Good Master"* to go unchallenged, so to speak, then some of His followers would ultimately ascribe that same thing to other teachers. In essence, He was proverbially nipping a possible problem in the bud.

Second: considering that Jeremiah wrote that *"the heart is deceitful above all things, and desperately wicked"*, then there's only one way to a pure heart; and that's by way of the Spirit of the Lord. But, I want to take a look at it from a slightly different viewpoint. Jeremiah was writing that our heart is full of dross; and the Lord said that it needs to be purified; exactly the way gold and silver is purified. And that is?

> *Behold, I will send my messenger, and he shall prepare the way before me: and the Lord, whom ye seek, shall suddenly come to his temple, even the messenger of the covenant, whom ye delight in: behold, he shall come, saith the Lord of hosts.*
>
> *But who may abide the day of his*

> *coming? and who shall stand when he appeareth? for he is like a refiner's fire, and like fullers' soap:*
>
> *And he shall sit as a refiner and purifier of silver: and he shall purify the sons of Levi, and purge them as gold and silver, that they may offer unto the Lord an offering in righteousness.*
>
> *Then shall the offering of Judah and Jerusalem be pleasant unto the Lord, as in the days of old, and as in former years. (Malachi 3:1 to 4)*

Yes: it's the Spirit of the Lord Who purifies our heart; but, He does it in ways that many times we sorely wish He wouldn't. We go through situations that stress us physically, we deal with people who try us, we go through times of deprivation; and then there are times when everything seems to be going well for us, when we're riding high, when we have what we need, and when everything is dovetailing. Yet, in EVERY situation, the Spirit is purifying our hearts.

> *But I rejoiced in the Lord greatly, that now at the last your care of me hath flourished again; wherein ye were also careful, but ye lacked opportunity.*
>
> *Not that I speak in respect of want: for I have learned, in whatsoever state I am, therewith to be content.*
>
> *I know both how to be abased, and I know how to abound: every where and in all things I am instructed both to be full and to be hungry, both to abound and to suffer need. (Philippians 4:10 to 12)*

It was through everything that Paul experienced in his life that he learned how to set his heart to accept whatever the Lord required of him. As a matter of fact, in verse 12, Paul said that he was <u>INSTRUCTED</u> to go through times of fulness, and through times of hunger; to go through times when he abounded, and times when he suffered need. Consequently, <u>THAT'S</u> the purity of heart that the Lord desires us to have. He isn't looking for us to necessarily do all things according to our preconceived notions of what it means to be a Christian, nor is He looking for us to be sugary sweet in every situation that we find ourselves in. Rather, the purity in heart that He wants us to seek for is the absolute desire to follow Him, to obey Him, to love Him, to honor Him, and to live wholly for Him. <u>THAT</u>, then, is how we attain to goodness in His eyes. And there's only one way that we can attain to the purity of heart.

> *For I will take you from among the heathen, and gather you out of all countries, and will bring you into your own land.*
>
> *Then will I sprinkle clean water upon you, and ye shall be clean: from all your filthiness, and from all your idols, will I cleanse you.*
>
> *A new heart also will I give you, and a new spirit will I put within you: and I will take away the stony heart out of your flesh, and I will give you an heart of flesh.*
>
> *And I will put my spirit within you, and cause you to walk in my statutes, and ye shall keep my judgments, and do them. (Ezekiel 36:24 to 27)*

Now, even though this was definitely speaking about a time in the latter days, it still has a present-day application. You see, the Lord HAS taken us out from among the heathen (the world), and HAS brought us into our own country (His Kingdom). He's also cleansed us from all of our past filthiness, given us His Spirit, and is in the process of changing our heart. In essence, He's giving us a heart transplant.

There's a condition that some people have, which is called "Hypertrophic Cardiomyopathy". This is where the heart muscles become abnormally thick and firm, which results in a reduction in the ability of the heart to pump the blood. According to doctors, this is hereditary. Can you see what I'm talking about here? Simply: in the natural, the condition of a thick, firm heart is passed on through the family; and, because it's something that many are not aware of having, then they're unaware that they have a possible life-threatening condition. It's the same in the spirit. People have spiritual "Hypertrophic Cardiomyopathy", wherein they have a hardened heart toward God in varying degrees. It's a hereditary condition, received from our first parents; and it's an eternal life-threatening condition!

There are some, however, who have received a new heart; and it's a pure heart, whereby they seek after the things of God. They want nothing else, and He only is their all in all. Thus, in His eyes, their heart is pure, and they're good according to what He calls good.

Faith, And The Peacemakers.

There are a couple of things in this portion that I want to address; and they're a little different than many believers think.

The first has to do with faith. Now, whenever we

think of faith, we tend to think of it in the sense of what we exhibit when we accept Jesus as our Lord and Savior. And, yes: that's a very necessary faith. Without it, we'd never be able to respond to the Spirit when He reached out to us.

As a matter of fact, that's something that we need to understand about just basic salvation. There are a lot of believers who are under the impression that it's our responsibility to reach as many of the unsaved as possible; and that's the focus of all of their attention and efforts. Now, I'm not discounting this, because they're doing what they feel that the Lord would have them to do, and the Lord definitely honors that. However, whenever we do what we believe to be the work of the Lord, we'd better make sure that it's what the Lord would have us to do. Let me give you an example.

> *Now when they had gone throughout Phrygia and the region of Galatia, and were forbidden of the Holy Ghost to preach the word in Asia,*
>
> *After they were come to Mysia, they assayed to go into Bithynia: but the Spirit suffered them not.*
>
> *And they passing by Mysia came down to Troas. (Acts 16:6 to 8)*

Paul, and those who were with him, intended to enter into Asia, and then into Bithynia, to preach the Word of God to those who were lost.

But the Holy Spirit refused to allow it!

Wasn't that an act of disobedience to the command that Jesus gave: *"Go ye into all the world, and preach the Gospel to every creature" (Mark 16:15)*?

But wasn't it the Holy Spirit Who refused to allow

it?! It makes no sense to those who hold to the idea that we have to reach as many people as possible with the message of salvation.

There's something that we need to realize, even in regard to basic salvation. We have to bring that ONLY TO THOSE to whom the Spirit of the Lord directs us. You see, there is a specific time for every person to be drawn to the Lord; and the Spirit knows this. For example, there was a specific time for Paul to be blinded by the light, and to be saved. He wouldn't have learned what He did of the law and the prophets, nor would he have gained the notoriety that he did, had he been converted before that time. Thus, he gained the knowledge that he needed, and the absolute proof that Jesus can save to the uttermost. Now, the vast majority don't experience such a drastic conversion; but, the bottom line is, the time of the offering of salvation to each one is set by the Father; and the Holy Spirit is the only One Who will draw them. So, the ONLY thing that becomes our responsibility is to allow the Spirit to direct us to whomever He will, and then to obey His prompting.

That, then, concerns the simple faith that leads to salvation; but, that's NOT the faith that we see as a fruit of the Spirit. Rather, it's the faith that surpasses reason, which, sadly, far too few Christians have. Take a look in the eleventh chapter of the book of Hebrews. It's the faith that Enoch had, who believed that he didn't need to experience physical death. It's the faith that Noah had, which he kept for 500 years, that allowed him to stay true to building the ark, though he had never seen rain, nor had any concept of what a flood meant. It's the faith of Abraham that not only caused him to leave his family and land, to go where he was commanded, but also caused him to believe God's promise of an heir who would come forth from him and Sarah when it was physically impossible. In other words, the entire eleventh chapter speaks of a company of people who had that special kind of indomitable faith that surpassed the simple faith that most believers have.

So, is that kind of faith something that they just picked up one day? Is it something that suddenly appeared, when they just woke up one morning, and decided to believe God without reservation? It isn't too hard to realize that it didn't happen that way. But is it something that they all spent their entire lives working on, and perfecting? Again: no. There's only ONE way that this kind of faith comes; and that's through the Spirit of God. It's a special faith that very few believers possess; and the only way that they receive it is through a close, dedicated, personal relationship with the Father.

This isn't OUR faith in action; it's the faith of Jesus Christ that supernaturally strengthens us when we know that we couldn't go any further, or when we find ourselves in a life or death situation. It's the kind of faith that the Father would dearly love every one of His people to seek for. However, He's aware that very few will. That's the reason that He had the author of the letter to the Hebrews include a detailed account in the eleventh chapter, so that it might spur some to seek after that kind of relationship, and that kind of faith.

Now, turning to what we read in the Beatitudes concerning *"the peacemakers"*, there's something that we need to understand about this particular word, and how it's directly connected with the faith that I was mentioning. You see, when we think of peace as a fruit of the Spirit, we tend to think of something along the lines of what I had spoken about a number of pages back. There, it held the connotation of being at peace with our enemies, be it through strength, or through mercy. In other words, the focus of that peace is personal. In this, however, the word *"peacemaker"* holds the connotation of reconciliation, and, specifically, reconciliation with God. So, in a sense, it's bringing peace between enemies.

> *For he is our peace, who hath made both one, and hath broken down the middle wall of partition between us;*
> *Having abolished in his flesh the enmity, even the law of commandments contained in ordinances; for to make in himself of twain one new man, so making peace;*
> *And that he might reconcile both unto God in one body by the cross, having slain the enmity thereby: (Ephesians 2:14 to 16)*

Jesus was the One Who reconciled us to the Father, when we were once at enmity with Him, and when we were His enemies. Yet, there are those who will come forth in His exact likeness; and they'll do the same things. There are countless multitudes who are enemies of the Father. But this company of people will minister reconciliation to them; and they'll attain peace with the Father.

So, how will this be accomplished? Well, I've heard it said that, if the emperors in the Roman Empire who sought to eradicate Christianity had refrained from persecuting them, the outcome might have been very different. That's because, when those who were called Barbarians witnessed the strength, and especially the peace, that Christians exhibited when they were being tortured and executed, then the Barbarians knew that there was something greater in the God of the Christians than in their gods; and Christianity grew by leaps and bounds. In other words, the believers ministered reconciliation, or peace, by the peace that they exhibited through the supernatural faith of Jesus Christ that was bestowed upon them. Take a look at the following portion of Scripture.

> *Insomuch that they brought forth the sick into the streets, and laid them on beds and couches, that at the least the shadow of Peter passing by might overshadow some of them. (Acts 5:15)*

In essence, Peter had to give the people his agenda for the day, so that they would know which direction he was going to be walking. That, then, would allow them to lay the sick along the street where the sun would cause Peter's shadow to fall upon them. But, then, they couldn't do anything at noon, when the sun was directly overhead, because there would be no shadow in any direction. Along with this, if Peter was walking, and the sun was in front or behind him, then, that too, would cause a problem.

Actually, that entire train of thought causes a problem. You see, we need to realize that the shadow that emanated from Peter was not a literal, physical one, but a spiritual one. In other words, Peter had such an anointing of the Holy Spirit that it went forth from him, just exactly like a shadow from the sun. And it was this emanation which healed all those upon whom it fell.

Can you understand that, even today, the Lord's Spirit <u>CAN</u> work through us, if we allow Him the freedom to do so. Though we don't have anywhere near the kind of anointing that Peter and Paul and all of the early church fathers had, we <u>STILL</u> have an anointing of the

Spirit, nonetheless. And even that portion of the Spirit can do amazingly miraculous things; and, most of the time, we're totally unaware of it! As long as we've received the baptism in the Holy Spirit, and He dwells in us, then He emanates from us more often than we know. We walk into the grocery store, and He touches those around us. We go to work, and He ministers to the needs of those with whom we come in contact. We speak to someone, and we say something that ministers to that person; and neither one of us are aware of the work that He's doing.

So, many believers think that the ministry of reconciliation requires us to be able to speak just the right words, or to do something profound, that captures the attention of others; with the result that they surrender their life to the Lord. Yes: there comes a definitive time with every person who has ever accepted, and ever will accept, the Lord; and it happens more often than not when the Gospel is presented to them. But never, with literally every single person, has it ever been an event. Rather, it's the work of preparation by the Holy Spirit over their entire life, from the moment they're born; and it includes countless times of unrecognized ministration through countless numbers of people who have no concept that anything was happening!

Meekness, And Those Persecuted For Righteousness' Sake.

Previously, I've taken a look at the fruit of meekness; so, I'm not going to go into any depth about it. The only thing that I want to mention again has to do with the fact that true meekness is the ability to learn to accept whatever the Lord determines for us. At the same time, I want to try to show how that meekness is related to the persecution that Jesus spoke about.

I want to ask you a question here. Now, many of us, as believers, attempt, to the best of our ability, to walk as the Lord wants us to. We do what we can to be good, upstanding citizens, to be honest, to treat others the way that we know the Lord would treat them, to work hard. In other words, we try to be His ambassadors, so that those around us can see Him. So, do we sometimes get a little confused about why some people not only fail to understand us, but actually go out of their way to oppose us? It seems as though there are more and more people intentionally walking a path that leads to destruction, and that they're doing that with their eyes wide open! As I mentioned earlier, Paul wrote about them in the first chapter of his letter to the Romans.

If we want to be able to walk as the Lord wants us to walk, then we'd better realize something here: this opposition is inevitable. Jesus spoke about that.

> *Another parable put he forth unto them, saying, The kingdom of heaven is likened unto a man which sowed good seed in his field:*
>
> *But while men slept, his enemy came and sowed tares among the wheat, and went his way.*
>
> *But when the blade was sprung up, and brought forth fruit, then appeared the tares also.*
>
> *So the servants of the householder came and said unto him, Sir, didst not thou sow good seed in thy field? from whence then hath it tares?*
>
> *He said unto them, An enemy hath*

done this. The servants said unto him, Wilt thou then that we go and gather them up?

But he said, Nay; lest while ye gather up the tares, ye root up also the wheat with them.

Let both grow together until the harvest: and in the time of harvest, I will say to the reapers, Gather ye together first the tares, and bind them in bundles to burn them: but gather the wheat into my barn. (Matthew 13:24 to 30)

It may sound like I'm simplifying things here; but, the sooner we become meek, and learn how to accept the fact that the wheat and the tares are growing up together, and that the Lord isn't going to remove them before His designated time, then we'll cease fretting and stewing, and we'll be able to do what He wants us to do without being drawn aside. Nothing swayed Jesus from His purpose, and we can't allow anything to sway us from His purpose for us. We <u>WILL</u> face opposition; and the closer to His Kingdom we get, the more fierce will that opposition be!

There's something that I noticed as I was writing that parable, and I want to bring it out here. In one way, it isn't directly connected to the point of this portion of the book; yet, at the same time, it adds to it. So, in the parable, Jesus said two things:

He said unto them, An enemy hath done this. The servants said unto him, Wilt thou then that we go and gather them up?

But he said, Nay; lest while ye

> *gather up the tares, ye root up also the wheat with them.*
>
> *Let both grow together until the harvest: and in the time of harvest, I will say to the reapers, Gather ye together first the tares, and bind them in bundles to burn them: but gather the wheat into my barn.*

On the one hand, the householder told his servants not to try to gather the tares out of the field, in case they unintentionally rooted up the wheat. But, then he said to wait, and in the time of harvest, the reapers would be able to take up the tares without rooting up the wheat. I don't know if you can see what I've seen. In that parable, there was a time when the wheat could be uprooted by trying to remove the tares, and there was a time when the wheat would hold firm. What the Lord is telling us is that, even though His people may be manifesting the fruit of the Spirit, and even though they may seem to be all that He's called them to be, they still need to go through the trials and tests that will come at the end of this age. It will be that time that will complete the work of firmly rooting and grounding them, so that the removal of the tares in the time of harvest will have no effect on them.

I have another question for you: what would be the cause of the wheat being uprooted by the removing of the tares? Well, by understanding what the wheat and the tares are, we'll get a better understanding of the effect that these things will have, and, consequently, why "the householder" made the decision that he did. You see, the wheat speaks of those who are true followers, and the tares speaks of those who are not. Pretty simple up to this point. But when we consider that wheat and tares look alike, then we can come to a conclusion. It isn't that, in attempting to remove the tares, the servants of the householder might have mistaken some wheat for tares. Rather, since the tares are those who appear to be wheat, then, should they begin to be removed earlier on, the effect on the wheat could be quite devastating, and could cause some of the wheat to waver, and to fall (to be uprooted). By waiting until the wheat has reached a point where they are fully aware of the purposes and reasons of the Lord, then, when those who are tares at heart are removed, the wheat will be able to accept His decisions without wavering; and they'll remain rooted and grounded.

So, we need to face the fact that, as believers, we WILL face opposition, both from nonbelievers, as well as from those who claim to be followers, but are not. The main reason that this will happen is what Jesus told us about.

> *And this is the condemnation, that light is come into the world, and men loved darkness rather than light, because their deeds were evil.*
>
> *For every one that doeth evil hateth the light, neither cometh to the light, lest his deeds should be reproved. (John 3:19 and 20)*

People hate to have their evil deeds exposed so much that they'll fight against those who manifest the light of the Lord upon them. We may fully intend to allow the presence of the Spirit of the Lord to manifest His love and grace toward them; but, in turn, they'll manifest an opposition and, sometimes, a hatred, in response. It may not make any sense to us, and we may be tempted to pull away from them, and to allow them to receive *"the reward of [their] iniquity" (Acts 1:18)*; but the Lord demands that we do as He did. After all, He was *"persecuted for righteousness' sake"*; yet He forgave, because He had learned to accept what the Father allowed to come His way.

Temperance, And To Rejoice, And Be Exceeding Glad.

As in the section about *"Joy"* and *"They That Mourn"*, this one, too, seems to be speaking about opposites. You see, *"temperance"* speaks of self-control; yet, then we see the Lord speaking about an excessive expression of joy. That, then, is why I put the two of them together.

You see, it may sound a bit strange, but there's really only one way that we can truly rejoice, and be exceeding glad, and that's if we have temperance. If we don't have temperance, then our rejoicing is based only upon our circumstances. How is that, you may ask? Well, temperance, like any other fruit, is a gift of the Holy Spirit; while, at the same time, it's also perfected through use. So, the more we make use of the fruit of temperance, the more that we're able to properly deal with whatever situation we find ourselves in. And, the more that we can deal with whatever situation we find ourselves in, then the more we can TRULY rejoice in what we know to be from the Lord's hand.

I've been in the work world for going on forty years, and I've noticed that most people have the same concept, and say the same things. When I've asked them how they were doing on most days of the week, their response has overwhelmingly been, "Well, I'm okay for a Monday, but that can change". And, on the last day of the week, it's been almost unanimously, "Thank God it's Friday". Unfortunately, many times this comes from those who claim that they're believers. We need to understand one thing: a good day should never be dependent upon our circumstances. If it were, then we'd be tossed to and fro, and we'd go from happy to sad to happy to sad. If we truly possess temperance, however, then, whatever situation we found ourselves in wouldn't overwhelm us, nor control our emotions. Thus, our rejoicing wouldn't be over what we consider "good" circumstances, and whether things are going our way. Rather, our rejoicing would be over what we know the Lord allows.

The Conclusion

I started this writing by looking at the fact that light waves which come from various celestial objects, such as stars, can be broken into its various components through the use of a spectroscope. By doing this, astronomers are able to determine what elements are present. At the same time, included in these are what are called Fraunhofer lines, which are areas in the spectrum that appear as dark lines; and they show what elements are missing. Through these, astronomers are able to determine what those celestial bodies are composed of, as well as a myriad of additional information.

In essence, those who are watching the heavens are able to determine a wealth of information about what they're watching through the light that comes from those objects.

So, we're being watched.

We're being watched by those around us.

We're being watched by family and friends.

We're being watched by coworkers.

We're being watched by neighbors.

We're being watched by people in the grocery store, in the post office, and in every place that we go.

And, then, we're being watched by the Lord.

We're being watched by the angelic realm of God, and of the enemy.

In other words, we're being watched at every moment, and in every facet, of our lives.

Do you know what they're all looking for, either knowingly or unknowingly?

They're looking for the elements that we manifest, to see what's in us, and what we're made of.

They're looking at the light that comes from us, and what makes up that light.

There are times when there are innumerable spiritual Fraunhofer lines, where we manifest the darkness of our spirit into our situations; and it does nothing but increase the confusion, and the tension, the discord, and the darkness. But there are other times when the light that we allow to shine through us is that which comes from the Spirit of God within us; and there are no Fraunhofer lines! You see, the light of the Spirit of God is a perfect light, with no lack, no darkness, not even a shadow of imperfection. And, yes: that light is within us even now. We may see ourselves as imperfect; and we are. But, for those of us who have allowed the Lord to take up residence within us, we also have the Holy Spirit of Perfect Light dwelling within.

It's our choice as to whom we allow to manifest in our lives.

If we give room to our spirit, then the manifestation of God's Spirit will be subdued, and the darkness that is in our spirit will overshadow all that we do.

But, if we give room to God's Spirit, then His marvelous light will shine forth unto all with whom we come in contact, and into every situation that we find ourselves; and the result will be the ministration of life and hope and glory!

All who have the Spirit of God dwelling within them have the capability of allowing the Lord to manifest through them.

All who have the Spirit of God dwelling within them have the capability of manifesting the fruit of the Spirit.

And all who have the Spirit of God dwelling within them, and who manifest the fruit of the Spirit, will, very naturally, be able to walk as Jesus spoke in the Beatitudes. It won't happen the other way around; because the fruit gives life to the manifestation of those qualities.

You see, the fruit of the Spirit are those elements which make up the Prism of God.

And it's this Prism that the world is waiting for.

That's because it's this Prism of God that is His promise to the creation!

> *And God spake unto Noah, and to his sons with him, saying,*
>
> *And I, behold, I establish my covenant with you, and with your seed after you;*
>
> *And with every living creature that is with you, of the fowl, of the cattle, and of every beast of the earth with you; from all that go out of the ark, to every beast of the earth.*
>
> *And I will establish my covenant with you; neither shall all flesh be cut off any more by the waters of a flood; neither shall there any more be a flood to destroy the earth.*
>
> *And God said, This is the token of the covenant which I make between me and you and every living creature that is with you, for perpetual generations:*
>
> *I do set my "Prism" in the cloud, and it shall be for a token of a covenant between me and the earth.*
>
> *And it shall come to pass, when I bring a cloud over the earth, that the "Prism" shall be seen in the cloud:*
>
> *And I will remember my covenant, which is between me and you and every living creature of all flesh; and the*

waters shall no more become a flood to destroy all flesh.

And the "Prism" shall be in the cloud; and I will look upon it, that I may remember the everlasting covenant between God and every living creature of all flesh that is upon the earth.

And God said unto Noah, This is the token of the covenant, which I have established between me and all flesh that is upon the earth. (Genesis 9:8 to 17)

[And] the "Prism of God" is love, joy, peace, longsuffering, gentleness, goodness, faith,

Meekness, temperance: against such there is no law. (Galatians 5:22 and 23)

Made in the USA
Middletown, DE
06 May 2022

65404562R00062